BASIC WESTERN TABLE ETIQUETTE AND WAITER SERVICE

BASIC WESTERN TABLE ETIQUETTE AND WAITER SERVICE

WAITER COURSE INCLUDED

Dr R C Bouer

AuthorHouse™ UK Ltd.
1663 Liberty Drive
Bloomington, IN 47403 USA
www.authorhouse.co.uk
Phone: 0800.197.4150

© 2013 Dr R C Bouer. All rights reserved.

No part of this book may be reproduced, stored in a retrieval system, or transmitted by any means without the written permission of the author.

Published by AuthorHouse 10/08/2013

ISBN: 978-1-4918-7943-6 (sc)
ISBN: 978-1-4918-7944-3 (e)

Any people depicted in stock imagery provided by Thinkstock are models, and such images are being used for illustrative purposes only.
Certain stock imagery © Thinkstock.

This book is printed on acid-free paper.

Because of the dynamic nature of the Internet, any web addresses or links contained in this book may have changed since publication and may no longer be valid. The views expressed in this work are solely those of the author and do not necessarily reflect the views of the publisher, and the publisher hereby disclaims any responsibility for them.

CONTENTS

The History Of Etiquette 1
The Waiter 2
The Value Of A Waiter 2
Code Of Conduct Appearance 3
Teamwork 6
Behaviour Of A Waiter... 6
Communication Skills.. 9
Non-Discrimination... 10
Trust And Honesty... 10
Spreading Of Disease 11
Safety And Security 12
Basic Responsibilities (Job Description)...................... 14
Preparation Before Opening.. 14
Check The Following 14
Answering The Telephone... 17
Meeting Guests At The Entrance Of The Restaurant 18
Serving The Guests... 20
Special Attention 32
Different Kinds Of (Serving)Entertainment 35
Banquet Service.. 35
Family Style Serving 36
(Buffet/Smorgasbord) 37
French Style Service... 39
Russian Service... 40
Amcrican Service.. 42
Cocktail Parties And Cheese And Wine Parties............ 43

Serving Tea 44
Important Information For The Waiter 46
The Menu 47
Setting The Table... 52
Standard Methods Of Setting A Table 66
Table Etiquette For Everyone 75
The Restaurant Guest 75
The Invited Guest.. 78
The Business Lunch... 90
Eating At The Workplace 90
Organize The Business Lunch.. 91

FOREWORD

This book does not claim to be the Alpha and the Omega of table etiquette. It fills the gap for the ordinary person such as you and I, who do not attend state dinners on a regular basis or at all. These basic etiquette rules are however, also applicable for state dinners as well as formal dinners.

We believe that we are very knowledgeable regarding the appropriate etiquette, and have a very good knowledge of good etiquette, and therefore it is good to confirm it. We, as parents often apply rules according to the way that we were taught as children not taking into consideration that our children were being brought up in a different environment of TV lunches and fast foods.

At home today's lifestyle does not provide for family to sit down at a neatly set table and have more than a one course meal served. Therefore parents are unable to set an example of table manners that they were taught as children. This book is about filling that gap and adapting to the different lifestyles which are relevant to our times.

Nowadays we dine out more than when we were children, and it is good to know what is expected from the guest and what the guest's perception is as well as what the perception of the waiter or restaurateur is. Notes in this book mainly deals with etiquette during mealtimes, in a Western lifestyle as well as with eating out at a restaurant. It does not deal with different cultures

Dr R C Bouer

where in some instances food is eaten with the hands or chopsticks etc. When food is eaten with the hands only, different hygiene and etiquette rules are applied.

This book also serves as a study guide for waiters. The evaluation questions that follow at the end of the book, gives the candidate an opportunity to qualify for a certificate in waiting. Instructions are supplied.

ACKNOWLEDGMENT

I wish to thank the Lord for opportunities and abilities.

Without the encouragement and support of my family, Rika, Ronel, Robert, Rachel and Henru and friends, Johan and Sonja, this book might still have been packed away somewhere in a cupboard.

I WISH TO EXTEND MY SINCERE APPRECIATION FOR THE ROYAL TREATMENT RECEIVED FROM THE MANAGEMENT AND STAFF OF:

AMAZINGWE LODGE
TEL: +0027 12 2058600

CASA GRANDE
TEL: +0027 829295688

THATCH HAVEN
TEL: +0027 12 2525028

LEOPARD LODGE
TEL: +0027 12 2071130

I would like to congratulate the author with a very knowledgeable piece of work. The educational value will have a far more reaching effect than just etiquette and waiter service.

You can use the book to educate a child and remind a Minister of Parliament about table protocol and etiquette.

I will recommend this book to each and every household.

Prof A. A. Basson

Dr R C Bouer

Doctor of NSc. (Univ. of Stellenbosch)

Doctor of Sc (Honoris Causa) (University of Colombo)

The author gave the reader . . . from all walks of life . . . from young and not so young . . . . information that will educate us to eat and enjoy food with confidence in public and with our family and friends. A must read! Congratulations!

Prof Potgieter D D PhD (USA)

THE HISTORY OF ETIQUETTE

Etiquette is the word given to expected human behavior in the social world.

The most important rule of etiquette is to behave in such a manner that you will not embarrass people in your company.

When people in your company do not apply the "correct" manners or behaviour you have to respect their behavior without comment or correcting them. "No word said, is no harm done" The only persons you are allowed to correct, would be your own children and then it is done at home and not in public or in front of their friends.

What is allowed in some cultures may be totally unacceptable in another culture. In some cultures when you "burp" after a meal it is a sign that you have enjoyed the food. In Western culture it is absolutely not allowed and considered as very bad manners

The word etiquette derives from the old French word "Ticket"

Etiquette is important to be socially accepted and at ease.

Etiquette does change with times and culture, but certain basic etiquette rules will never change.

Each state has a special department, assisting his officials and visitors pertaining to each country concerned are protocol. The word protocol is used instead of etiquette.

The first known notes on etiquette were written about 4.500 years ago.

It was customary for a father to write notes of conduct to his son or for a leader to write notes of behavior to his subordinates.

Etiquette covers all the areas of our lives.

There are sets of etiquette for almost every aspect of life e.g. in relationships, cellular phone use, weddings, at hotels, parties, travelling, home entertaining, living in commune, hostel, graduation ceremonies, in business and any other situation that you can think of.

A. THE WAITER

THE VALUE OF A WAITER

The waiting staff is the core of the business. Proper training is the key to a motivated waiter. You need some basic knowledge to be a good waiter and become an indispensable asset to the restaurant.

You, as the waiter could make a good impression, to the extent that clients would like to come back to the same restaurant because of the good service, or stay away because the service was disappointing. That is why it is of the utmost importance that management selects the right person to trust his valued customers to. Clients will, in most cases hardly have any contact with the chef or management, and the waiter is the only person that represents them. Some guests do not report bad service, but you can be sure they will talk and these rumors can put any restaurant out of business.

A good waiter is the main link in establishing a good customer base.

A good waiter is the best advertising investment any restaurant could ever have.

It is said, as a fact, that 69% of clients are lost due to the attitude or indifference on the part of an employee.

CODE OF CONDUCT APPEARANCE

DRESS CODE

At some restaurants a standard uniform is prescribed. At all times the attire worn by the waiter should be scrupulously clean. The uniform should be without wrinkles, spots or stains. This is the first impression the guest will have and it will reflect the standard that can be expected from the rest of the restaurant. There should be as little detail possible on the uniform and it should fit well and be comfortable to wear. Sleeves should not be too long and hang over the hands or too wide that it brushes over the food. The clothing should never be revealing. Wear clean comfortable shoes. The waiter is on his/her feet the whole day. Take good care of your feet, wash it daily and wear clean stockings or socks.

It is a good idea to wear a name tag, pinned in a conspicuous place and large enough to enable the guest to see it easily. It is good for the guest to identify the waiter and call him/her by name.

JEWELLERY

A waiter should wear the least possible jewelry while serving. No tingling bracelets or long necklaces that may dip into the food are allowed.

You may wear only one ring. The waiter has to wash hands regularly and cannot take off a number of rings all the time. Dirt and bacteria accumulate under the rings.

GENERAL HYGIENE

The waiter must make sure that he/she looks fresh and clean throughout the shift. Take a bath/shower daily. Use a proper deodorant. Be careful not to use strong smelling perfume or spray that fills the room when you enter. Men must shave daily. Women should wear moderate make up.

Mind your breath. Do not eat strong smelling food such as garlic or drink beverages such as alcohol that could result in bad breath. The chewing of chewing gum is not allowed, and will not clear the breath of the waiter.

It is expected from a waiter not to smoke. Non smokers cannot tolerate the smell of smoke, which could cling to the clothes and hair of a waiter. It is a sure put-off for a non-smoker to see the waiters hanging around outside the restaurant, having a smoke-break. Washing your hands will not take the cigarette smell from the clothes and hair.

THE HANDS OF THE WAITER

The attention of the customer is always on the hands of the waiter. Your hands tell a story of your personal cleanliness. Your hands should be clean and free of blisters or sores. If this is the case, have it well covered or wear gloves until such sores are healed. Your nails should be clean, short and well cared for. No nail polish is allowed as it easily becomes chipped when the waitress needs to wash her hands more often than usual. Do not wash hands in the area where food is prepared. Brush your hands and nails with a nail brush and an antiseptic soap and dry with air or disposable paper. Your fingers should never touch the inside of a plate, bowl, glass or cup. Hands should be washed after visiting the toilet, cleaning out used dishes, cleaning something from the floor or handling money.

HAIR

Hair should be permanently out of the face and precautions should be taken that it cannot fall into the served food. Long hair should be tied at the back. Wash your hair regularly and keep it clean and shiny. Choose a hair style that you need not correct continuously, e.g. brushing it out of your eyes.

TEAMWORK

The waiter forms one link in the chain of a team to ensure the harmonious flow of activities in the restaurant. A waiter should be able to take orders from co-workers and assist them whenever an opportunity arises. When the waiter is not waiting at a table it is good teamwork to assist in the kitchen, even if it is to help clean up or chop vegetables.

It will be expected from the waiter to communicate with the rest of the staff in the establishment. This will include management, the bartender, kitchen staff, bus boys and even the dishwashers and cleaners.

To be a good team worker the waiter must be a good communicator. He/she must be able to be a good listener, be able to give orders and to take orders. He/she must be willing and able to assist with any task, even out of his/her job description.

The waiter should have a positive attitude and phrases such as "I can't" "I do not think it is possible" "I will see if I have time" "It is not part of my job" should not be used by the waiter

BEHAVIOUR OF A WAITER

Before you become a waiter you should be acquainted with the basic etiquette rules. You must apply perfect manners and be well informed of what to expect from your guests and how they should (or are expected to) behave when you serve them. Serve your customer with a big smile and always be in a good mood while serving the customers.

The customer pays for good service and expects the best possible treatment.

Show the customers, by being professional and with good behavior that you are proud that they have chosen your restaurant and that it is an honor for you to serve them. When it is a customer you recognize as having been there before, greet him/her with a smile and say "so good to see you". Be friendly but not familiar

Diners mainly visit a restaurant to be "restored" (from the French word restore)—it is to feel good after visiting the restaurant and not only just to satisfy their hunger.

Mind your body language. Show interest and indicate that you are keen to serve them. Be enthusiastic without faking it. Say verbally to yourself as you greet customers entering, that these are great people and I am going to enjoy every minute while serving them to the best of my ability.

A waiter is not part of the party, but assists the customers in such a manner that, without them noticing it, the meal will go off smoothly. You might not even be noticed by the guest, but when you are not professional and the service is not good, you might be noticed, and this might/not be as positive as you could wish for.

The waiter should be proud of his/her work and when she/he treats the client with respect, the client will treat her/him with respect.

Never lose your temper or show emotion when you feel like bursting with fury from the inside. When difficult situations occur, concentrate on the issue and never become personal or take criticism personally. When you are waiting, you take on the character of a waiter. Even if you have a few degrees in another field, the client is only interested in good service. Treat each guest as the most important person you have ever come across, who knows this person could just be your next employer or recommend you to other important persons, because of your positive attitude. Do not inform your customers you only do waiting as a part time job, that you are a student or only doing to gain the experience.

Your mission is to be of service to your customers and this should be your objective until you leave your shift. No matter what your personal situation might be, it is of no concern. You must be polite and friendly. Another ill treatment from a customer should never upset you to the extent that you will not be able to continue with serving your other customers. A waiter should always be emotionally in control and not take uneasy or unfriendly comments from the guests personally.

Few people can really resist being rude to a waiter who is friendly and professional. When working with people you must expect to have to deal with all kinds and personalities. You will always be exposed to criticism and you have to be in control and be able to deal with all situations.

Always keep in mind the personal space of your clients. Do not stand too close to your client and never make any physical contact with your client. Do not stretch over one client to serve another client at the other end of the table.

A professional waiter should ignore excessive attention from the client and even more so from someone of the opposite sex.

A waiter should not pay extra attention to the person who is paying the bill with the expectation of receiving a larger tip. It might just annoy the other guests and place them in an uncomfortable position. Such a customer will soon ask to be served by another waiter. Your guests should be put at ease in any situation that is in your power to control.

Ask a waiter close to you to keep an eye on your table if you need to leave your table for a while. Absenteeism is one of the most frustrating issues any restaurateur can experience. If you really cannot attend work, make sure you personally notify the manager by telephone or by messenger and also in good time so that the manager has time to make alternative arrangements. Your manager must know that he can depend on you and that you can even stand in for an emergency. This is vital for you to build a positive work record and a reference in future on your C.V.

COMMUNICATION SKILLS

Good communication skills are of most importance for becoming a good waiter. This might need some study to be applied at the work place. You must be able to "read" your guests. This will be developed as you are focused on the needs of your customers. You could be more informal without becoming personal or less professional with a group of young people and more formal with a group of business men. You will be able to tell when it is a business meeting, when they are seriously in a conversation. Do not disturb them by asking "is everything in order"

Be careful to do upselling if you see the client cannot afford more courses or extra orders. Try to identify the host or the person who is going to pay the bill. They should give you an indication who is going to pay the bill. Be observant when they give you hand signs as to whom you should give the bill. Keep an eye on the table and react on any hand signs that they indicate they need your attention. Observe their facial expression which will indicate when they are content or not with your behaviour.

Part of good communication skills is to be a good listener and to answer questions. Give information needed and not more.

NON-DISCRIMINATION

You have to treat all customers with the needed respect and professionalism. You should not treat people differently whom you think is of a lower income, or a gender you do not like, or of a different race.

TRUST AND HONESTY

Honesty is highly valued in any person employed. This characteristic is even more important when you are employed as a waiter. There are so many areas where your honesty will be tested.

When customers leave some of their items behind, take all the precautions you can to return it to the customer. If you are very busy, take the items to management and report where and at what table it was found, as well as their names, if the customer gave details when making the reservation.

When you have broken or damaged anything, report it.

Take special note that the correct change is given to the client and do not keep any change back or take it for granted that it could serve as a tip.

Do not serve more to the client than what they pay for, with the expectation to gain their favor and receive a larger tip. Watch out for intoxicated guests who expect favors from the bar and kitchen and do not want to pay for it. A manager with experience will not take long to assess whether you are an honest person or not.

A trustworthy person will keep confidential information to him/herself. Activities in the establishment should not be discussed with outside persons, unless it is good advertisement. When promises and commitments are made, it must be honored. Do not perform hard work and extra hours with the expectation to be rewarded. Your trustworthiness will be noticed. If you are not promoted, it might reflect on your CV.

SPREADING OF DISEASE

When you have a cold or any kind of contaminating disease, you are not supposed to serve food. Coughing and sneezing is not permitted while serving food. Take note that you have no unhygienic mannerisms such as scratching your nose, ear or correcting your hairstyle continuously. A waiter should never chew chewing gum or eat while serving customers.

Do not lick your fingers. It is not acceptable to use a tissue and to blow your nose while serving. Do it in the bathroom. Do not serve guests with utensils that have been on another table where guests were seated. You do not know if it has been used. Dispose of all left-over food. Some guests might have some disease and serving left-over food to someone else might spread diseases.

Dispose of any used paper serviettes and remove other serviettes immediately and place it in the proper laundry bin.

Extra utensils are handed to guests on a tray. When cutlery is carried without a tray, hold it folded in a serviette; it is only more professional and hygienic.

When you notice any ants, cockroaches, rodents or any unwanted insects report it immediately to management.

SAFETY AND SECURITY

Acquaint yourself with all the safety rules and adhere to it in the restaurant. Observe the safety signs. Make sure you know where the fire extinguishers are, where the emergency outlets are, in case of a fire breakout. Make sure you know how to operate the safety equipment and that it is in good working order. You must know who the appointed first aider is on the staff, in case a client needs immediate attention for minor emergencies such as a burning wound or a cut with a knife.

Keep passageways, working areas and serving routes clear of all obstructions.

Always be on the watch out for guest coming in and out and children running around.

Clean up immediately when something has been spilled, even if you did not spill it. Pick up any litter and items out of place.

Check for broken and default equipment, e.g. chipped or broken glasses or other utensils, remove and replace it.

Carry utensils on a tray, especially sharp knives. These should be folded in a serviette and brought to the table on a tray. Do not carry too much crockery to the table at one time, rather walk twice and prevent plates or dishes from falling.

Whenever there is an emergency, always save lives first. Give the alarm. Keep calm and assist customers and staff to leave the venue. When there is a robbery, do not play the hero. Try anything so you will be able to identify the robber later. Look for scars on the face, hands, eyes etc.

Inform management immediately when any incident occurs that you cannot handle.

When a glass has been broken, be careful when picking up the pieces, warn customers, watch out for any pieces that could have landed anywhere else, further away from the scene. When someone gets hurt, assist where you can or call management to take over. You are not a doctor and cannot give advice to customers. Report to management immediately when you have broken any item or when it is broken by a customer.

Warn your clients when you serve anything that is piping hot. Do not serve very hot food or food on overheated crockery to children.

BASIC RESPONSIBILITIES (JOB DESCRIPTION) PREPARATION BEFORE OPENING

Arrive early enough to be prepared and at ease when you start your shift.

In each restaurant the stations (tables or settings for a group of people) to be served, will be assigned to each waiter. Tables are usually numbered to assist the waiter with the serving.

Check on the booking register and acquaint yourself with the guests you expect at your station or tables.

CHECK THE FOLLOWING

SERVING ENVIRONMENT

All tables and chairs should be in its proper place with all chairs correctly arranged. All tables assigned to you must be ready and set up for service. Even when busboys (people setting the table and removing the used utensils from the table) are appointed to see to the tables, the waiter must still make sure everything is in order.

Tables must be correctly set for the number of guests who have made a prior booking. See that there are enough chairs or a baby chair if needed.

Tablecloths and serviettes should be free from stains and creases. Tablecloths should hang evenly over the table. Serviettes should be neatly folded and placed for each customer.

Move the chairs away from the table and check if the seats are clean. Check under the tables and chairs for pieces of food or bubblegum. Check if the table is well balanced and level.

TABLE ARRANGEMENTS

Take care that flowers on the tables are not wilted or the previous night's half burned candles were left on the table. Artificial flowers do not fall in good taste. The flowers or other table arrangements should not be too large or obscure the view of guests on the opposite side of the table. Take care that the table does not become too crowded with unnecessary items.

AMBIENCE

Music

Music should not be too loud. Loud music will make guests feel uncomfortable and disturb their conviviality. This will cause the guests to ask for the bill and leave earlier than planned, and these will not recommend the restaurant to their friends. No music on the other hand, could create a formal and slightly uncomfortable atmosphere.

Take care that the air conditioners are in good working order and that a comfortable temperature is maintained in the restaurant during summer and winter time.

Odors in the restaurant

Make sure the tables nearest to the rest room are not so close to the restroom that guests could be embarrassed by bad odors coming from the restroom. Visit the restrooms on regular basis to see that everything is in order and that it is deodorized.

Check the tables nearest to the kitchen door /area to ascertain that strong odors e.g. roasted garlic do not bother the guests.

THE SIDE STAND

Check the side stand nearest to your station. All the necessary items should be at hand for immediate service e.g. ice tongs, ashtrays, lighter, clean napkins, sponges and towels, order pads, pens, toothpicks.

Fill up the salt and pepper canisters; check if the holes are open.

Clean the brims and bottles used for mustard, tomato sauce from finger marks or pieces of food. Check if the sauces are fresh and not stale. Replace when empty or almost empty.

The serviettes should be clean and neat. Placemats, menus, china, silver cutlery and glasses should be clean and have no spots or even finger marks on them.

Make a note of anything that can save you an extra trip or to run around while serving customers and add it to your daily check list to keep on your side stand to be of aid with your serving. You could hand your list to the busboy to check and keep up to date during meal time when you are busy serving.

Check your menus. It should be clean and not torn.

ANSWERING THE TELEPHONE

TELEPHONE ETIQUETTE

No telephone should ring more than three times without being answered.

Ask someone whom you can trust to evaluate your voice and voice tone when you answer the phone.

Do you talk as if you are tired, not interested, unsure, and too soft or too fast etc.?

Answer the phone by saying:"This is the Royal Restaurant, Sam speaking. How may I help you?"

When a booking is made, see that you have taken down the following information:

- Name of the guest
- Telephone or contact number of the customer
- Number of guests to be expected
- Number of adults and number of children
- Baby chair needed
- Date of booking
- Time of booking
- Preference of seating: smoking, side, centre.

A booking list with all the relevant headings could assist the receptionist or waiter with the booking of the client. Make sure that all the information is given through to management in order to prepare for the expected guests.

Provide detailed information about the restaurant's policies and operations, e.g. code of dress, bringing their own liquor, making their own music, mode of payment, as some restaurants do not take cash and some do not take cheques.

You have to handle sales calls. Make sure the information is taken and conveyed correctly to the person concerned, e.g. special events or take away meals.

Route telephone calls to the proper source when you do not have the information they need. In some cases it might be a message for one of the guests. Take messages and do not forget to give it to the person concerned.

MEETING GUESTS AT THE ENTRANCE OF THE RESTAURANT

The maître d' meets the guests at the entrance. If the restaurant does not make use of a maître d', the waiter should meet the guests. It is not a good idea for all the waiters to line up at the entrance when the restaurant is not busy. The waiters, who are not serving, should be appointed to meet the guests.

When the guests enter the restaurant they need to receive immediate attention. When they enter, meet and greet them with a smile. Be relaxed while you make eye contact with them. Make the introduction as brief as possible. Good eye contact indicates undivided attention and portrays confidence. You should not be talking on the phone or be busy doing something else and then just lift your head to greet them. Give them your undivided attention.

Accompany the guests to their table which is reserved for them. At this stage the maitre'd or hostess should hand the guests over to the waiter if the waiter did not escort them to the table.

Introduce yourself.

Waiter: "Good day, my name is John, and I will be your waiter today."

Allow the guests to be seated before you communicate with them again.

Address your guests as Sir, Ms or madam, but never Mrs. or auntie or uncle. Never call them by nicknames such as "lovie"," my dear" or "dolly". It is not professional and is in bad taste. When a guest is alone ask how many people would be joining him/her, never ask: "Are you alone?"

Make sure before opening that you know who made reservations and where they are to be seated.

SEATING

When a booking has been made in advance it should appear in your booking register. Sometimes restaurants paste a booking chart at the entrance. This makes the customers feel welcome the minute they enter.

Show them to their tables if they have booked. If they did not book in advance, ask them where they would like to be seated. Assist the elderly, the ladies, the children and the disabled to be seated. Always pull out a chair for the elderly or a lady. The gentlemen are supposed to assist the ladies. Stand back and allow your guest to be seated. Place children where they will also enjoy their meal but will cause the least disturbance to the rest of the guests. Caution the elderly to mind steps and take the space into consideration when seating a disabled person in a wheel chair.

SERVING THE GUESTS
PRESENTING THE MENU

Before you present the menu, make sure everyone is seated.

Ask if you can serve someone with water. Present them with a wine list and ask if you could call the wine steward to take an order and serve them with something from the bar.

The menu and your attitude are your main sales tools.

Stand on the left side of the guest when taking the order.

Hand out an open menu to each guest if it was folded.

The menu is presented from the left side of the guest. Hand the first menu to the host, then to all the guests, ladies and the elderly first, moving in a clockwise direction around the table.

SALES SKILLS

You have to practice the skill of "suggestive selling". You can only apply suggestive selling if you are well acquainted with the menu and the foods served at the restaurant. You can guide the guests by making suggestions regarding tasty dishes on the menu. This skill does not always apply as some customers have already decided what their choice will be.

Practice not to ask questions with: "yes" or "no". E.g. "Would you like some coffee?" or "Can I bring you something to drink?"

Each question should at least suggest an order e.g. "What would you like me to serve you from our bar?" or "Would you like a whisky or for the ladies a sherry before the wine is served?" "I recommend our nutty chocolate milkshake for the children".

Ask your customer if they will allow you to introduce them to some tasty dishes on your menu. Explain briefly to arouse their interest and whet their appetite. When you have regular customers, it is a good idea to remember their names and take trouble to remember the names of their children.

Inform them about the special offers your restaurant has. You would like to cater for them for birthdays, celebrations, or any special occasion. Suggest items that will compliment their meal. Never be too pushy to force expensive items on your customers. "Read" your clients to determine their needs.

UPSELLING

When the customer is interested in a dish, you may offer to serve certain accompaniments to the dish. You must inform the customer that it will come at an additional cost. Suggest that they could choose a double milkshake instead of an ordinary milkshake. Do this very discreetly, as the client could feel uneasy if you impose more and expensive items to be ordered.

SERVING OF BEVERAGES
THE WINE STEWARD

The wine steward must be a specialist on wines, the serving of different kinds of beverages that is available at the restaurant. The wine steward could suggest an appropriate wine to be served with a certain dish. Never try to be more informed and wiser that the guests, unless your advice is asked. The choice of the customer must always be respected, never overrule or criticize their choice. This is a specialized field that we do not cover in this book.

Sometimes the waiter needs to assist the guests with the serving of the wine or other beverages. The waiter should observe the laws of the country and not serve alcohol to under aged, even with the permission of the parents, as the management of the restaurant must adhere to the law.

Learn as much as you can about the serving of wines and all the different wines available served at the restaurant. Check the stock in the cellar so that you know if a certain kind of wine required by a customer is available. If not, you can suggest a similar kind of wine. If guests need to wait for their table, they may be served with drinks at the bar or lounge. The waiter must assist the guest to take their unfinished drinks to their table, when their table is ready.

When wine is served, the bottle is presented to the host for his approval. The host should feel the temperature of the wine taste it and show his approval to the waiter. White wine should be chilled and red wine served at room temperature.

Make sure the correct glasses are used for the kind of beverages ordered. All wines are opened at the table. When red wine is served, the cork should be presented to the host to smell, to make sure that it is not musty and the wine is of good quality. The waiter should pour a little wine for the host to taste (or for the person who has ordered the wine) the guest should show his approval.

The waiter can now serve the rest of the table with wine, starting from the lady on the right side of the host, then the guest at the head of the table, moving in a anti-clockwise direction, serving the host last. Keep an eye on your guests and fill up their glasses when it is empty and when they indicate that you can fill up their glasses.

White wine is kept on ice and red wine is placed in a slanted container. The glass or cup is left in its position as it is set, and the waiter should pour the drinks from the right side of the guest.

When you pour from a bottle, turn the bottle as you stop pouring to prevent the beverage from dripping. Never fill up glasses or cups to the brim.

Make sure that you hold a clean, dry cloth next to the hot container e.g. when glühwein is served to protect the customer.

Pour sparkling or gas beverages holding the glass in the hand by the stem, slightly slanted and then pour the beverage, by running it down the side of the glass.

When a different bottle of wine is ordered, remove the used glasses and replace with clean glasses. Never fill glasses more than two thirds with white wine more than half full with red wine. Always ask first before you top up the wine glasses. When a bottle is empty, ask the host: "Would you like to order the same, or try another wine?" Some beverages such as beer are never recommended by a waiter, as it is too filling and not a good choice before a meal. When the guest orders beer the waiter should serve the beer without any comment.

TAKING THE ORDER

Stand on the left side of the guest when taking the order. Stand at a comfortable distance away from the guests. It can be very embarrassing if a waitress stands too close and it is difficult for the guest from his position, being seated, to look the waiter in the face. Do not stand too far off, where you have difficulty hearing what the guest says. Be careful of too intense eye contact, this could also make your guest feel uncomfortable.

Give the guests enough time to decide. Stand at a distance and ask them to call when they are ready to order. Take the order of the host first, or the order of the elderly first, following with the lady next to the host, and then in an anti-clockwise manner until all orders have been placed. You must have your notebook and a sharp pencil or pen in your hand. (Make sure the pen can write)

Try to make use of shorthand notes and try clues by which to remember your guests and what they have ordered, such as hair, glasses, plus minus age 20 or 50 m=man or f=female or red tie. Do not number them in the order they are seated, as they may change seats. Make up your own codes such as 0 for potato or o for rice or// for chips, etc. Make sure the chef understands your codes thereby making sure the order is understood. It is easy when the items on the menu are numbered, but guests will always have special orders which are not on the list.

Repeat the order to confirm that what you have noted is what they ordered. It is a good idea to write the order using a carbon copy, if the note book is not in duplicate. If you have to give the original to the kitchen staff you have a copy to refer to. It is embarrassing for the waiter to have to ask who ordered what.

Indicate to the guests more or less how long the preparation per dish will take.

EXPEDITER

"Expo" is the abbreviated term for expediter. The function of this person is to receive the orders from the waiters and hand it to the kitchen staff and to receive the prepared orders from the kitchen and hand it to the waiters. The expediter has to make sure that the food ordered is prepared according to the order given and that the temperature of the food is correct. It is still the responsibility of the waiter to make sure the order he/she receives is correct, before taking it to the guests.

SERVING

Remove all the menus and the extra glasses or cutlery from the table after taking the order.

If possible, try to serve all the guests at the same time. It would be a good idea to have other waiters assists you into delivering the whole order at the same time to all the guests. It is never a good idea to serve some guests first, and allow them to wait for the other guests to receive their food because by the time everyone is served, the first guest's food might be cold, or if they start eating before everyone is served, the first one will be finished by the time the last guest is served.

When the kitchen staff indicates that your order is ready, do not take it for granted that everything is in order. Check the order before you take it to the table. Ladies and elderly people are served first and then the rest.

Basic Western Table Etiquette And Waiter Service

Make sure that your hands do not touch the food when you are serving.

Note that the dishes that are to be served hot are dished up on pre heated plates. Make sure that the food which is supposed to be served hot is hot and food supposed to be served cold is chilled.

Place the food from the left side of the guest onto the table in front of the guest, with your right hand. Try not to stretch over the other guests. In a booth, the customer at the furthest end is served first, in order not to stretch or pass the food over someone else's food. Where possible, assist the guests with young children. Remember you are not a babysitter, so more is not expected of you.

Keep a constant eye on your groups, as they will indicate when they need your attention. Be very careful never to interrupt a conversation by asking "is everything all right" Sometimes the guest has food in his/her mouth and it might be embarrassing to swallow the food quickly in order to answer the waiter. Rather inform them that you will be around and they must feel free to indicate when you can be of service.

Make sure there is an extra plate when food such as unpeeled prawns or spare ribs are served, as well as finger bowls, serviettes and hot damp finger cloths.

Supply extra serviettes for children.

WAITING TIME

Indicate to the guest how long each dish ordered would take more or less to be served. Read your customers. If they are there during lunchtime from work, they might only have an hour and cannot wait 30 minutes for an order. You must learn to "read" your customers. If they are there to enjoy the whole evening at the restaurant, you may suggest some hors d'oeuvres before the meal. Too many customers are lost, due to the timing of the kitchen and waiter.

DESSERT

At the end of the meal, you have to ask your guests if you could serve them dessert, liqueur, coffee etc. It has become custom to drop a few peppermints with the bill. The waiter could give each guest a peppermint chocolate or something special. The guests will be surprised and remember the "grand finale".

Introduce your guests to the dessert after the meal. Even if they have to share portions, it is better than no order at all. Ask by saying "Why not order one dessert to share, only to taste our specialty dessert?"

Do not forget the no-go, yes or no answer. Do not ask "Do you want tea or coffee?" Offer the coffee by asking "would you like some coffee with brandy or a liqueur?" Do not ask "white or black coffee?", rather "coffee with cold, hot or without milk"? If they do not help themselves to milk, do not fill the cup more than two thirds.

SMOKING

Have a lighter at hand to assist guests to light their cigarettes. Clear the ashtrays before the main meal is served or when you see it is necessary. Ashtrays are removed by covering the dirty ashtray with the clean one. Remove both from the table and replace the clean ashtray on the table. The waiter needs to practice changing the ashtrays as quickly as possible.

CLEARING THE TABLE (CRUMBED-DOWN)

When all the guests have finished with their course, you may remove the used plates from the right side of the guest. If you are not sure that they have finished, rather ask than presume that they have finished. When there is still food on the plate, even if they have placed their knife and fork vertically, see if the other guests are still busy and make no attempt to remove the plate, unless they indicate that they want it removed. When guests place their knife and fork next to each other in vertical position, it is to indicate they have finished. Do not always take the rule for granted.

When you are clearing crumbs from the table, make sure you have a tray or something to wipe the crumbs from the table. The crumbs should not be wiped from the table onto the floor or chairs.

ACCIDENTS AT THE TABLE

Take special notice if one of the guests has an accident. Assist them immediately with no great ado and trying to attract the least attention. Apart from being a good waiter, good manners are always appreciated. One gesture which will always be appreciated is when you endeavor to spare someone an embarrassment.

Without making a fuss, you can replace the serviette when the guest has used the serviette to clean up a mess.

CONVERSATION WITH YOUR GUESTS

Keep conversation restricted to servicing. Do your utmost to answer questions in the most professional manner and to make no conversation about yourself. Make sure or find out the correct answers if general questions are asked. Answer them objectively. When guests expect more attention from you than needed, quickly excuse yourself politely. When a situation gets out of hand, ask someone else to take over your table. Do not take notice of conversations at the guest's table. Should you hear something that might interest you, you are not supposed to discuss it with no one, as it was not meant for your ears.

THE BILL

Adhere to the system used by the restaurant. Most restaurants have their own system of payment. It is the responsibility of the waiter to acquaint him/herself with the in-house system.

Try to determine who will be responsible for paying the bill. Make sure that there is no mistake on the bill. Hand the bill to the host on the appropriate container or side plate, upside down. Always return the correct change, even if it is a few cents. It is the prerogative of the guest to leave you a tip; it would be arrogant of you to take it for granted that you may take the change.

CREDIT CARD DENIED

Be discreet and make no great deal of it. Casually ask for another form of payment. Do not use the words; "denied" or "declined". Your customers should always feel comfortable and appreciated. You could tell your guest to come and assist you because your system does not want to read the card. Explain the situation to the customer and never confront a customer in front of the other guests. When the customer has no alternative method of payment, you have to hand the situation over to management.

GREETING

When they leave, assist your guests e.g. put on their coats, check that they did not leave something behind. Assist with the children when needed. Greet with "it was such a pleasure to service your table" or if there were some unfortunate situations: "although we had some misunderstandings, you have taught me a few lessons that I can rely on in the future".

SPECIAL ATTENTION

CHILDREN

See that children are seated where the mother can easily attend to the child. Place a high chair at the table where it will not bother other guests. Without a fuss, remove any breakable items, salt, pepper out of the child's reach.

Never take an order from a child without the consent of the parents. Supply extra napkins, disposable bibs for babies, novelty place mats or whatever the restaurant has to offer for children.

When children run around in the Restaurant, ask the parents in a friendly way to keep the children at their tables because of safety reasons, and you would not like the children to get hurt. They might bump into waiters with hot food or crockery. You are not to attend to children while the parents are enjoying their meals; your work is to serve the guests.

Never fill any beverages to the brim for children or serve them food that is too hot. Allow the parents to assist the children and give them cutlery suitable for small children. They will know if the little ones can handle a fork or a spoon. You may be asked to serve the children with food which can be prepared immediately if you notice the children are becoming impatient.

PHYSICALLY IMPAIRED GUESTS

Place guests in wheelchairs in the most safe and comfortable place and not where it will be too conspicuous that they need extra space.

Treat the physically impaired person as normal as possible. Read the menu to the blind. Allow the deaf persons to indicate what they need and never try to overrule them.

You may touch the blind customer slightly on his left shoulder, to indicate that you are passing the food at the right shoulder to indicate that you are serving beverages or removing used utensils.

ALLERGIES AND SPECIAL NUTRITIONAL NEEDS

When the guests indicate that they are allergic to some ingredients, you have to take it into consideration when you take the order. For you to be able to assist your guests in this regard, you must have knowledge of all the ingredients of the dishes you serve.

ACCIDENTS AT THE TABLE

When an accident occurs or when a guest chokes, ask someone with experience to assist the guest. The appointed first aider should take care of minor ailments, but otherwise the family of the guest in trouble should react. You may assist to call an ambulance. The manager should always be informed of any such an incident.

INTOXICATED GUESTS

When you notice that the guests have had too much alcohol to drink and they are becoming a nuisance to the other guests, you may ask them to move to another place in the restaurant where they will not bother other guests when they are noisy. Make sure that they have paid the bill before they leave. Whenever the situation becomes difficult for you to handle, report it to management.

SPECIAL REQUIREMENTS FROM GUESTS

Sometimes the guest might ask you for something e.g. from the chemist, or some direction to some place, or some hotels, go out of your way to assist them. Provide language assistance for foreign speakers where possible.

COMPLAINTS FROM GUESTS

There will always be guests who complain. It is part of your work to eliminate situations, as far as possible, for them to complain about. When they are not satisfied with something, you have to apologize immediately and see how you can correct the situation. Sometimes you have to compromise e.g. if the dish has to go back to the kitchen because it is not according to their order, you may offer an appetizer or bring extra bread without charge. You have to deal with the situation in such a manner that they need not report it to management. Discuss with management what they would allow you to do to keep the customer happy, should such situations occur. Your mistakes could cause the restaurant suffering losses, if you have to hand out freebees for your mistakes.

DIFFERENT KINDS OF (SERVING) ENTERTAINMENT

BANQUET SERVICE

Banquet service is a formal method of entertaining a large group of people with full set cover. (With all the silver needed). A set menu is served by waiters with all the relevant courses and each course is more or less served at the same time to all guests. Serving is according to the American style. One waiter serves not more than two or four guests during the meal.

The food is dished up garnished or decorated in the preparation area for each guest. The chef places the plate of food in front of the guest. An under plate should be set for each guest so that the cover should not be empty while waiting for the next course.

At the entrance of the banquet room a diagram must indicate the guests where to be seated. Name cards are set to indicate the position of each guest at the table.

Etiquette

Etiquette or protocol rules are to be strictly observed. Guests are only allowed when invited and guests should reply on the invitation, which is usually formal.

No eating with the hands and no second helpings. Use the correct crockery and cutlery. Eat as far as possible the food that is served to you. Do not decline any of the courses, unless you are allergic to food served. If you are not hungry, you may eat a portion of the food served. When different wines are served with different courses, take care not to drink too much.

You do not have to empty each glass of wine served.

FAMILY STYLE SERVING

Food is prepared and sliced in the kitchen and is put onto the table for each member of the family to help themselves. Food is passed from one person to the one next to him.

Etiquette

At home in the family, family rules are adhered to. Family members should respect one another. The mother would usually assist the children first. Each member would serve themself. Consider other family members. Consider the amount of food in the dish and the number of family members to be served. When there are only six potatoes in the dish and six members to be served, one person should not take more than one potato. Use a different spoon to dish up the food. Imagine if the same spoon is used to dish up

Basic Western Table Etiquette And Waiter Service

beetroot and rice. Only when all members are served, second helpings are allowed.

(BUFFET/SMORGASBORD)

Buffet served in Sweden meaning table of sandwiches

The different dishes are arranged on a table. Covers are set for guests at a different table. The plates are arranged on the table with the dishes. Guests are seated at their allocated tables. The guest would order their wine and then serve themselves. Buffet meals are also accompanied with a carvery. The meat is sliced, carved by the chef at the buffet table and guests choose the cut and portion size.

This style of service is used for barbeques where food is prepared outdoors and then served to the guests. Meals served outdoors are referred to as "al fresco".

Etiquette

At a buffet, guests serve themselves. The guests will be seated at their set tables. They order their wine or beverages from the wine steward. After the wine is served, the guests move to the table where the food is arranged. Most of the time at a buffet table, the starter is arranged at a separate table. Heated plates are supplied. When this is the case, the guests dish up the starter. After the starter is enjoyed, the waiter will remove the used plates. The guest will now dish up the main meal and after this the dessert. We do not pile food on top of another. Serve yourself with small portions. Finish all the food you have dished up and only then go for second helpings. Do not scratch around in the serving dishes and try to disturb the garnish or decorations as little as possible. Do not scoop off all the cheese from the au gratin or dish up all the decoration cherries for yourself, only because you like cherries. Use a different spoon for different dishes.

Dish up moderate portions. Half a chicken is not a moderate portion. No food is taken home at a buffet meal. The waiter will remove the used plates from your table. Do not put used utensils on the table where the food is arranged.

When guests queue up to serve themselves, make sure you keep a safe personal space and consider other guests. Do not push or bump into guests or show impatience when some guests take longer to serve themselves than you think is needed. Assist where you can.

FRENCH STYLE SERVICE

French style serving is also called table top cooking. The main chef (Chef de rang), an experienced chef prepares the food at the table with the guests observing. The food is usually partially prepared and the final preparation is done at the guest's table. The Chef de rang usually has an experienced assistant, called the Commis de rang. A small spirit stove (rechaoud) is used to keep the food warm. A gas flame is used to prepare the dishes.

A Flambé dish

(Food with alcohol poured over and set to flame) is a popular dish to serve and done while the guests are overlooking

Etiquette

Guests should order flambé dishes in advance; because it needs extra time to pre cook the dishes and two chefs are needed to serve. Guests should not be in a hurry and pay attention to the preparation, as this is part of the entertainment. Show the needed appreciation to the chefs.

RUSSIAN SERVICE

This is a formal method of serving with only one waiter serving. The waiter places the empty plates in front of each guest. The waiter then brings the food in a serving dish and dishes a portion of food onto the plate of each guest.

The waiter serves from the left side of the guests and counter clockwise around the table. The waiter returns the serving dishes with the leftover food after all guests have been served.

Etiquette

The guests should indicate to the waiter the portion size and kind of food he/she prefers. Move only slightly away to make space for the waiter to dish up your food. The waiter will collect the used plates. Do not hand the plates to the waiter. He knows what to do and it could only cause confusion. Never forget to thank the waiter when he serves you.

AMERICAN SERVICE

American style is less formal and most commonly used in restaurants. Salad, bread and butter is placed on the table. The food is dished up in individual plates in the kitchen and the waiter brings the plate to each guest. The used plates are removed from the left. Beverages are served from the right. Food is served from the right and used plates are removed from the left side of the guests.

COCKTAIL PARTIES AND CHEESE AND WINE PARTIES

This is an informal way of serving small or large numbers of guests. No formal table is set for individual guests. Guests stand and serve themselves. The meal usually starts at 18:30 to 19:00 and should not last longer than two hours. There are no seating arrangements for the guests. For a cheese and wine, a variation of cheeses, biscuits and dips are set out and only wine and fruit juices are served.

At cocktail parties different kinds of drinks are served. The guests help themselves at the table where variations of individual, easy to serve foods are arranged. The preparation of food is such that guests can eat either by hand or with a toothpick or a cocktail fork e.g. sausage rolls, samoosas, canapés etc. No knives and forks are supplied. Waiters move amongst the guests and serve snacks or drinks. Throughout the duration of the party, the waiters must clean up as inconspicuously as possible by removing used glasses, used serviettes, toothpicks and other used items from the room. The waiters must also fill up empty platters and keep the table with the food as neatly arranged as possible.

Etiquette

Guests help themselves. Try not to fiddle with the food while you dish up for yourself. Do not touch food you do not intend to place on your plate. Do not pile up the food on your plate. Do not place more than four items on the small plate. Rather go for second helpings than to have an overloaded plate. Help yourself with something to drink or receive it from the waiter. When you have finished your drink, help yourself to the food. You cannot eat with a glass in the one hand and a plate of food in the other. Start with something savoury and then something sweet. Do not place your used utensils or serviettes on the table with the food. Observe where a place has been made available to place used glasses and plates. Do not place glasses on the floor where it can be bumped over. When there is a dish you like, do not place half of the dish onto your plate and leave none for the rest of the guests.

No take-aways are allowed at a cheese and wine or cocktail party.

SERVING TEA

Serving tea could be formal or informal. Tea-time is between breakfast and lunch and between lunch and supper.

"High tea" is not considered as an important or a formal tea, but rather as a light meal served with tea.

A tea party should not last longer than two hours. A tea party may be organized in different ways, according to the occasion.

The following factors will influence the method of preparation for a tea party.

- Time of the day
- Number of guests
- Kind of occasion
- Facilities available

A morning tea is usually served between 10:00 and 12:00.

Tea and coffee is served. Light refreshments such as small sandwiches and scones with cream and jam can be served.

The afternoon tea is served between 14:00 to 17:00. Tea and coffee is served. If needed, champagne may be served, depending on the occasion. Richer cakes and pastries are served for an afternoon tea. This is also considered as "high tea".

Number of guests

For a large number of guests tables can be set in conjunction with self-service.

Etiquette

The guests need to be guided by the hostess. The hostess would pour and serve the tea or indicate that the guests serve themselves. Do not help yourself before the hostess has been served. Never use your own utensils for dishing up, e.g. use the sugar spoon to scoop the sugar. Do not use the sugar spoon to stir your tea/coffee. Use the serving utensils to dish up e.g. a slice of cake. Sandwiches and dry biscuits are eaten by hand. First have some cake or sandwiches, and then pour the tea. If sweet and savory items are served, first eat the savory and then the sweet items. Place the used serviette unfolded, on the small plate or on the tablecloth, not inside the used cup.

Never drink coffee or tea from a cup or a mug with the spoon still inside. Hold the cup or mug by the ear and not with your hands folded around the cup.

Do not lick the spoon. The doily on the saucer is supposed to absorb the excess moisture from the cup or spoon to prevent tea from dripping while you drink.

IMPORTANT INFORMATION FOR THE WAITER

Each restaurant/hotel will have its own set of rules and the waiter has to acquaint himself/herself as soon as possible with the in-house rules.

A waiter should obtain as much information as possible to be able to conduct his/her work successfully. Find out in the kitchen from the chefs and in the dining room from the busboys how different tasks are performed and why. Remember knowledge is power. Someday you might even be a CEO of a large company and then these basic rules and knowledge will still be relevant.

THE MENU

Some guests may be allergic to some ingredients or might not eat some foods because of their religious beliefs. If guests cannot determine the ingredients by the name of a dish you must be able to inform them accordingly. When a Muslim requires halaal food, the chef should also be informed accordingly. Most Jews would not eat food with any pork in it. Vegetarians do not eat any kind of meat.

Spend time in the kitchen to see how each dish is prepared and what kind of ingredients is used. You must make a point of tasting the dishes to enable you to inform the guests how you liked the dish. You should never tell a guest that you did not like a dish, as your taste might differ from that of the guest. Ask the chef what alternatives you could suggest in case a guest should ask you. Find out how long each dish takes to be prepared to guide you when you have to tell the guests what the waiting time would be. Study the menu and memorize it. Any salesman should know the product he/she is selling. Find out if you can serve different foodstuffs required by the guests, which do not appear on the menu, as well as how it would influence the bill. If it comes at an extra charge, you can inform your guest accordingly.

SPECIAL ITEMS

Sometimes special prices for some items are presented to boost the sales. It is your duty to inform your guests. Tell them that they should take note that on a Friday the oxtail will be at a special price.

SIGNATURE ITEM

A signature item refers to the specialty item of the restaurant on the menu. This could be a particular dish that was created by the restaurant and for which it is is very well known. This specialty item, the (signature item) should always be on the menu. A great signature item is the best way to advertise the business and draw customers. A good waiter should always "sell" the signature item first to the guests.

KINDS OF MENUS

A la carte	each item on the menu is ordered separately and paid for as the price indicates.
Table d'hôte	any or all the foods on the menu may be ordered and only one price is paid for the full menu.
Buffet	All items at the buffet table are listed, guests help themselves and usually one price is paid for the full menu. Normally no menu is presented to a guest at a restaurant when a buffet is served.

Cooking Methods

Dry methods of cooking

Baking	Cooked in an oven
Grilling	Cooked by the direct heat of a griller or hot coals.
Roasted	Cooked by direct heat, usually in the oven.

Broiling	Cooked by direct heat in a broiler or on a griller, basted with oil.
Braised	Browned with little oil and then cooked slowly with a little water which is continuously replenished.
Fried	Dry fried: food fries in its own oil e.g. bacon.
	Shallow fried: food fried in a little oil e.g. fried eggs.
	Deep fat fried: Food fried in deep fat/oil which covers the food e.g. fried potato chips.
Sauté	Food is cooked by tossing it in a little hot oil or fat.

Moist cooking methods

Boiling	Food cooked in water e.g. boiling of rice.
Stewing	A slow method of cooking in a little water, e.g. stewing of tough meat cuts.
Poaching	Food cooked in la little water or milk, e.g. haddock, eggs.
Pressure cooked	Food is cooked by steam under pressure.
Simmering	Foods cooked in a little water, similar to stewing.

Some dishes are cooked with a combination of methods, e.g. braising

Foods cooked in a microwave oven.

Most of the time foods are precooked and quickly heated to serve to the guests.

WAITING TIME FOR YOUR GUESTS

Find out from the kitchen staff how long each dish listed on the menu would take to prepare. Some dishes have already been prepared such as soup or stews, and only need to be heated in the microwave oven.

Some dishes are partially prepared while other dishes need to be prepared right from the start when ordered by the guests.

ACCOMPANIMENTS

Accompaniments are important to compliment a dish as well as add variety and make the dish more interesting. Sometimes accompaniments are served to disguise or control side effects of some ingredients e.g. parsley is served with a dish containing garlic to disguise the smell of the garlic.

Guests will indicate the accompaniments they want. Other guests will take it for granted that the waiter will serve the correct accompaniment with the food ordered.

The following are some traditional accompaniments:

- Horseradish sauce and Yorkshire pudding are served with roasted beef.
- Apple sauce or cranberry jam and mustard are served with pork.
- Sour cream with baked potatoes.

- Mint sauce or mint jelly with leg of mutton.
- Cream and syrup or ice cream with waffles.
- Lemon and Tartar sauce with fish.

A variation of condiments and accessories are placed on the table or passed to the guests from the sideboard such as mustard, tomato sauce and chutney.

Different sauces such as mushroom, garlic, cheese or other sauces are prepared by the chef. Introduce these sauces to your guests.

GARNISHING

Savoury (salty) foods or dishes are garnished with savoury garnishes such as parsley, vegetables or any other suitable items.

DECORATING

The term used for sweet dishes or Food such as desserts or cakes which are decorated and not garnished. It is usually decorated with items such as flower petals, mint leaves or any suitable items, but not with parsley.

SERVING DISHES

Each restaurant uses its own kind of serving dishes. Some restaurants serve food in a frying pan. It might be suitable for fish, but not suitable to be used with a knife and a fork, as the side of the pan is too high. When the pan is hot it could also cause a problem.

Steaks are served on a hot iron plate to keep the steak warm. A wooden plate is placed under the iron plate to prevent the guest from burning. Food is mainly served American style at most restaurants. The waiter has no say as to which plate the food is served on, as the dishing up is done in the kitchen.

Always ask your guests if they are comfortable to have their food served on a pre-heated plate. Some customers might just prefer not to have a heated plate. Warn the customer if the plate is hot and place it in a comfortable position in front of your guest.

Be very careful when you inform your client about the portion size of a dish. The menu should indicate the portion size. Explain the size of dishes such as pasta dishes, Bobotie or Shepherd's pie. Inform the guests about the choice of starches to be served as well as vegetables and if it is included. Whenever any item is to be paid for separately, the guest should be informed accordingly.

SETTING THE TABLE
TABLE LINEN

The table can be set with a full tablecloth or with place mats.

Under liner

A table liner is placed under the tablecloth. Any smooth thick material is suitable such as felt, batting, artificial leather.

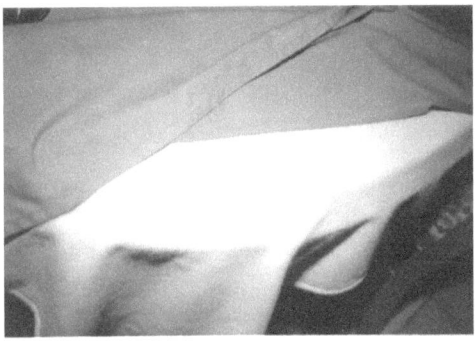

The function of an underliner is to dampen the noise of the cutlery and crockery and it protects the table. A lovely table top such as marble or wood may be exposed by the use of table mats.

Table cloth

The tablecloth is important and could play an important role in your colour scheme. The tablecloth should hang evenly over the table but not more than twenty cm on the sides and should not rest on the chair. Any kind of material is suitable as long as it is not too rough so that the glasses can stand firmly.

Server plate

This plate is placed on the cover and the plate of food is placed onto it. It is mainly used at banquets and formal dinners.

The server plate or under plate plays an important role in the decoration and color scheme of the table arrangement.

The most important function of the under plate or server plate is that when different courses are served, that the cover should not be empty.

Serviettes (table napkins)

Serviettes should be made of absorbable material. A serviette has a decorative and functional purpose. It forms an important part in the decoration and colour scheme of the table.

The serviette can be folded and placed on the server plate or on the left of the cover on the side plate, folded or in a serviette ring. Sometimes serviettes are placed in one of the glasses to serve as decoration or folded in different fancy shapes.

The more formal the occasion, the larger the serviette. The size of a serviette varies from 350mmx350mm to

600mmx600mm. A serviette does not always need to be square. Material serviettes should always be used and paper serviettes are only used for take away meals and children's parties, but are not a good choice for any other meal.

At formal dinners the waiter places the serviette on the lap of his guest. Only children are allowed to use their serviette as a bib. As soon as the meal starts at formal dinners, when the host or hostess has placed his/her serviette on his/her lap, the rest of the guests should do the same, if the waiter did not do it for them.

Finger-bowl

Sometimes a pile of paper serviettes are used with a finger bowl. A special finger bowl-cloth, sealed in a plastic wrapping is supplied. The cloth must be damp and heated in a microwave oven. In some cases an ordinary dry serviette is used with the finger-bowl.

Dr R C Bouer

CUTLERY

History

Cutlery is also referred to as flatware.

Knives were used 3000 years ago and it was made from hard stone, mainly flint stone. In the early Middle Ages knives and later forks were made from precious metals such as gold, silver, enamel, even gems, marble and mother-of-pearl. These forks were mainly used by the nobility and wealthy people of the day.

During the 13th century the nobility and wealthy would bring along a box, called acadena, with their own personal fork and spoon.

Different utensils were used such as the Knork—knife and fork.

Spork: A spoon and fork combination. Spife—a spoon and knife.

The cutler's trade developed since the industrial revolution and advanced in a full scale manufacturing business.

Cutlery was first made of animal horns with skin hide and wood for handles. It was only during 1913 to 1935 that stainless steel was used in the manufacturing of cutlery.

Knives

Different knives are used to set the table, each with a different use.

- Table-knife:

The knives are made of silver or stainless steel.

The table-knife is larger than the dessert-knife. Knives are placed on the right side of the cover (plate) with the cutting side facing the plate.

- Dessert-knife:

The dessert knife is placed next to the table knife, on the right side or outside. The dessert knife is sometimes placed on the left side of the cover, on top of the side plate. The dessert knife is used to spread butter and jam on bread, and not to cut the bread, bread is broken with the hands. After the bread has been spread, the dessert knife is placed on the side plate and left there till after the meal.

- Steak-knife

The steak-knife has a serrated edge and is served with all kinds of steak. It is not usually set at the table, but brought to the table when steak is served.

- Fish-knife

The fish knife is blunt and used for fish that is easily sectioned into smaller portions. The fish knife is set on the right side of the plate, in the order of serving.

- Butter-knife

The butter knife does not form part of the cover or individual setting, but serves as a serving-spoon for the butter when a whole piece of butter is placed on the table. Do not use your individual setting to scoop butter from the butter dish, but use the butter knife and place a piece of butter on the side plate. Replace the butter knife for the other guests to use.

Do not hold the knife in your fist or like a pen. Never lick the knife and never put the knife in your mouth.

When you are not using the knife to eat, place it horizontally on your plate.

Forks

There are about 30 different kinds of forks used in the household, we discuss only a few in everyday use.

- Dinner-fork

The table fork is larger than the dessert fork and placed on the left side of the cover with the tines of the fork showing upwards.

- Dessert-fork

The dessert fork is smaller than the dinner fork and is placed at the top of the plate; handle to the left side, nearest to the plate.

- Fish-fork

The fish fork is similar to the dessert fork, blunt and slightly curved on the one side. Used with the fish knife to eat fish.

- Hors d'oeuvre fork

This fork is much smaller than the dessert fork and used to eat the hors d'oeuvres. It could be set next to the soup spoon on the right, or above the dessert spoon. Sometimes it is not set on the cover, but served with the hors d'oeuvre.

A fork is always used with the tines facing downwards. The knife is used to scoop the food onto the fork. When food such as peas is eaten, the peas may be mashed with the fork and then scooped onto the back of the tines. When only a fork is set, it may be used with the tines showing up, e.g. Bobotie or Shepherd's pie. When eating spaghetti, only a fork is used. Traditionally the spaghetti is whirled around the fork, holding the tines on the plate. Sometimes it is preferred to hold the tines against a spoon while whirling the spaghetti around the tines of the fork.

The fork should never be used to scoop up a large portion of food and then be eaten portion by portion from the fork. Never lick food off the fork.

- Fondue forks

A fondue fork is used to cook the pieces of food in oil. When it is dipped into the oil to cook, another fork should be served with which to eat the food, as the fondue fork would be too hot to be used to eat from.

Spoons

• Soup-spoon
The soup-spoon is round shaped. The soup spoon is served on the right side of the cover, next to the dessert knife, or in order of service. Soup is scooped up from the front to the top of the plate and sipped from the spoon. The whole spoon in not put into the mouth as is the case with a dessert spoon. Sip the soup without making a noise and do not lick the spoon.

• Dessert Spoon
The dessert spoon is shallow and oval in shape. The dessert spoon is used to eat porridge and puddings. Scoop only enough food on the first half of the spoon and put the spoon into the mouth. Never overload the spoon and lick or eat only some of the food in portions from the spoon.

When a dessert is eaten with a spoon, the dessert fork is used to clean the underside of the spoon by moving the fork tines down from the front to the back side of the spoon.

• Teaspoon
The teaspoon is smaller than the dessert spoon but larger than the demitasse spoon. The spoon is used to stir coffee or tea or to eat sorbet. It is set in order of the menu. When a teaspoon is placed on a saucer for tea or coffee, the spoon should lie on the right side of the ear of the cup.

• Serving cutlery
Serving cutlery should always be observed and used correctly. The guest should not use his personal cutlery to dish up food. The serving spoons are usually larger than the dessert

spoon. Use a separate spoon for each dish. Use a butter knife for butter and a jam spoon for jams and jellies. Use a cheese knife to cut a portion of cheese. A soup-ladle or a gravy ladle should be supplied to serve soups and gravies. A separate saucer should be supplied to place the used serving spoons

Salt and Pepper

Salt and pepper cellars should always be supplied to the guests.

For formal dinners, each cover should be set with salt and pepper. For any other item not set on the table, just ask for it.

Finger bowls

A finger-bowl filled with hot water, not piping hot that might burn the guest. Inside the water a slice of lemon may be placed. Together with the finger bowl extra serviettes and sometimes heated serviettes are served.

Finger bowls are served when food is eaten with the hands, e.g. unshelled prawns, crabstick, spare ribs and some fruit. Only dip the fingers into the bowl and not the whole hand. The finger bowl is set on the right side above the knives.

Coffee and tea

Coffee and tea or other hot beverages are to be served on a saucer. On the saucer a doily is placed of absorbable material (never plastic). The purpose of the doily is to absorb any drops of beverage and prevent it from dripping on the guest's clothes. The function of the doily is to absorb spilt liquid and staining is of no account. The spoon should be placed in line with the handle of the cup, on its right side. After stirring the teaspoon must be removed and placed back in the saucer. In the case of a mug without a saucer, the same rule applies. Do not lick the spoon clean. Do not blow the hot beverage to cool it; rather stir to cool it down. Never drink any beverage with the spoon inside the cup or mug. It is not acceptable to hold a cup with both hands. Hold the cup by handle.

Only dry rusks may be dipped into a beverage. Not even dry cookies are supposed to be soaked in the beverage. You are not allowed to sip beverages while eating. Swallowing down food with a beverage is viewed as bad manners.

GLASSES

Glasses are placed on the right hand side above the knife, in the order of serving. Only the glasses that are going to be needed should be placed on the table. For chilled drinks, glasses are held by the stem of the glass. Brandy-glasses are held with the ball of the glass in the palm of the hand. Red wine-glasses are held by the ball of the glass but white wine and champagne glasses are held by the stem of the glass. Do not lick the glass, if by accident it drips; wipe excess with your serviette.

For each new bottle of wine served, clean glasses should be supplied. Glasses are never filled more than two thirds full for white wine and half full for red wine, considering the size of the glass.

Not all glasses are discussed, such as martini, vodka etc.

Basic Western Table Etiquette And Waiter Service

Most of the following glasses are used during the serving of meals.

• Shooter
The shooter glass is flat and small, served at cocktail parties. Used for beverages high in alcohol and also for schnapps.

• Liqueur
It is a small glass with a short stem which holds 50ml to 100ml liquid and is used to serve liqueurs after meals.

• Sherry
The sherry glass is almost similar to the liqueur glass, but slightly larger and holds 75ml to 100 ml liquid. Sherry is served before meals but is high in alcohol. Sherry could be dry, medium or full. The same kind of glass is used for all kinds of sherry. Fill the glass only two thirds and not full.

- Port

The port glass is similar to the sherry glass. Port is served at the end of the meal, with fruit.

- White wine/Rose

The white wine glass holds 200ml to 250ml liquid. The white wine glass must have a stem as the glass must be held on the stem to prevent the hand from heating the wine. The glass should never be filled more than with about two thirds full. If it is a larger glass, no more than 200 ml of wine poured into the glass. Traditionally white wine is served with fish or white meat. Rose can be served with any kind of dish.

No ice cubes are served with white wine.

- Red wine

The red wine glass is larger than the white wine glass. Red wine is served with venison or red meat. The glass is never filled more than half full. Red wine is served at room temperature and is held with the ball of the glass in the palm of the hand.

- Cocktail

The cocktail glass is used for a variation of mixed cocktails. Cocktails are served at various informal occasions.

- Champagne

This glass is flute shaped, to preserve the sparkle and aroma. Served with any special occasion.

- Sorbet

The sorbet glass consists of a bowl which is filled with ice, with a separate bowl on top in which the sorbet is served.

- Whisky

Whisky is served at different occasions, but not served with the meal, but rather at the end of the meal when coffee is served.

- Brandy/Cognac

Brandy is served with or without ice, after the meal. The coffee is then usually served with or without sugar and milk; it depends on the taste of your guests.

CROCKERY

Different kinds of utensils are used to eat different dishes. In years gone by tableware was referred to as china and silver. Today in most households, mainly stainless steel is used for cutlery and crockery is made of china, porcelain, or pottery. According to the occasion, containers made of cardboard, plastic, polystyrene may be used, e.g. outdoor picnics or children's parties. Some cultures use communal dishes and all people would sit around the container with food and help themselves. Some cultures use banana leaves or other mediums to dish up their food. Different cultures have different methods of eating their food. Some only use their hands, other chopsticks. For our purposes we will discuss the use of knives and forks, used by the Western countries. During the 16th century Elizabeth I used a fork because the ruffs around her neck were so big that a fork had to be used to bring the food to her mouth.

A neatly set table is as important as the careful preparation of the food. If meals are always eaten on the lap while watching television opportunities are lost to teach our children basic etiquette.

STANDARD METHODS OF SETTING A TABLE

The way in which a table is laid is influenced by mainly three factors:
The kind of meal
Tradition
Menu

In some cultures it is customary to eat with your hand. In some cases only the left hand may be used and others only use their right hand. Make it your business to find out what the custom is so as not to offend any of your guests.

Enough space should be available for each cover (setting) from 40 cm to 60cm space is needed for each guest.

The necessary space, tables, chairs, linen, cutlery, crockery and glasses should be available.

Each restaurant will have its own special method of setting the table. At some restaurants a placemat, knife, fork spoon or any other utensil the guest might need is brought to the table as soon as the guest is seated or as soon as the order has been placed.

Forks are always set on the left side of the cover with the twines facing upwards.

Basic Western Table Etiquette And Waiter Service

Spoons are set at various positions depending on the purpose it is to be used for. The dome side of the spoon should be on the table with the wide side of the spoon facing upwards. Knives are set at different positions, depending of the purpose for which it is to be used. The cutting side of the knife should always face where the server plate will be placed.

The kind of food served determines how the table is set.

The cutlery should be evenly spaced in the space available and in a straight line, more or less 1 cm from the side of the table.

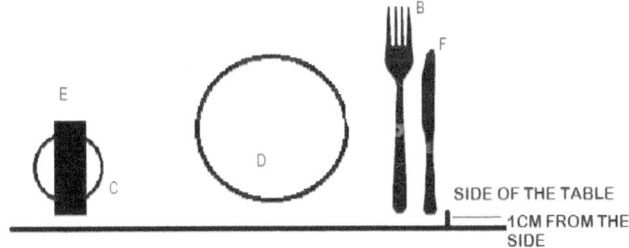

Fig 1

Fig 2

A-GLASSES
B-DINNER FORK
C-SIDE-PLATE
D-SERVER-PLATE
E-SERVIETTE
F-BREAD-KNIFE
ONLY ONE DISH IS SERVED

Curry and rice or bobotie where no knife is needed

- ONE COURSE MEAL

This is a meal where all food is dished up on one plate, with no other courses, e.g. meat, starch, vegetables, salad. The salad may be served on the side plate; bread is always served on the side plate.

Basic Western Table Etiquette And Waiter Service

FIG 3

A-GLASSES
B-DINNER-FORK
C-TABLE KNIFE
D-SIDE PLATE
E-SERVER PLATE
F-SERVIETTE
G-BREAD KNIFE (DESSERT KNIFE)

When spaghetti is served, a deep plate is set with only a fork and in some cases a spoon.

- TWO COURSE MEAL

A menu is served with meat, starch, salad, vegetables and dessert.

Dr R C Bouer

Fig 4

A-GLASSES
B-DINNER-FORK
C-TABLE-KNIFE
D-SIDE-PLATE
E-SERVER-PLATE
F-SERVIETTE
G-BREAD-KNIFE
H-DESSERT SPOON
I-DESSERT-FORK

- TWO COURSE MEAL

Main meal and soup

Basic Western Table Etiquette And Waiter Service

A-GLASSES
B-DINNER FORK
C-TABLE-KNIFE
D-SIDE-PLATE
E-SERVER-PLATE
F-SERVIETTE
G-DESSERT KNIFE/BREAD-KNIFE
H-SOUP-SPOON
- THREE COURSE MEAL

This could be a menu consisting of either soup or another kind of Hors'd oeuvre as the first course, the main meal with meat, starch vegetables, salad and a dessert.

For a Hors d'oeuvre the small fork may be placed on the small plate on the doily.

Dr R C Bouer

FIG 6

A-GLASSES
B-DINNER-FORK
C-TABLE-KNIFE
D-SIDE-PLATE (BREAD-PLATE)
E-SERVER-PLATE
F-SERVIETTE
G-BREAD-KNIFE (DESSERT-KNIFE)
H-DESSERT-SPOON
I-DESSERT-FORK
J-HORS D'OEVRE-FORK

- THE FORMAL DINNER

All the different courses may be served or only some of them. All cutleries do not have to be set, as some may be brought to the table as the different courses are served.

Basic Western Table Etiquette And Waiter Service

FIG 7

A-GLASSES
B-DINNER-FORK
C-TABLE-KNIFE
D-SIDE-PLATE
E-SERVER-PLATE
F-SERVIETTE
G-BREAD-KNIFE (DESSERT-KNIFE)
H-DESSERT-SPOON
I-DESSERT-FORK
J-HORST D'OEVRE-FORK
K-NAME-PLATE
L-SERVIETTE
M-FISH-KNIFE
N-FISH FORK
O-SOUP-SPOON
P-SORBET-SPOON

COURSES FOR THE FORMAL DINNER

1. Starter or hors d'oeuvre
This could be fish, served cold or hot, with a hors d'oeuvre fork, if not set out on the table. A variation of other foods,

such as fruit may also be served. This course is usually already placed on the server or served on a plate with a doily and is placed in front of each guest.

2. Soup
A soup spoon is placed, on the far outside of the server plate, with the dessert knife on the right side of the soup spoon or the dessert knife may be placed on the side plate at the left. The knife is not used to cut the bread, only to spread butter or jam.

3. Fish
The fish knife is placed next to the soup spoon, on the inside, nearest to the server plate and the fork is placed on the far side, on the left of the server plate.

4. Entrée
A table knife is placed on the inside of the fish knife on the right side with the cutting sides facing inside. The dinner-fork is placed on the left, next to the fish fork.

5. Sorbet
This iced palate cleaner, usually has a refreshing fruit base. A small spoon is served that is brought to the table when the sorbet is served. As sorbet is frozen fruit puree, you have to eat small spoonfuls at a time.

6. Main course
A table-knife and dinner-fork is used. If the table knife and fork is used for the entrée, a clean set of knives and forks are set for this course. The knife and fork is set nearest to the server plate.

7. Dessert
A spoon is set at the top of the server plate, handle facing to the right and the dessert fork is placed below the spoon, with its handle facing to the left.

8. Fruit/cheese/biscuits
Cutlery for a maximum of four courses is set. Any extra cutlery is brought to the table with each next course.

B. TABLE ETIQUETTE FOR EVERYONE THE RESTAURANT GUEST
RESERVATIONS

Make reservations in advance. Give the needed information to the restaurateur:

- Date and time.
- Number of guests.
- Number of children and number of adults that will be present.
- Position where you would prefer to sit in the restaurant: Private, side table, smoking or nonsmoking.
- If there are any special needs or babies, inform the restaurateur. Baby—a corner seat for the baby chair or wheel chair.
- Your contact numbers.

Entering the restaurant

- When entering the restaurant the Maitre'd would assist you, do not walk in and pick a table and be seated, it might be reserved and you will be humiliated to stand up and sit at another table.
- Tell her/him your name and the number of guests.

- Follow him/her to show you your table.
- Thank the Maitre'd for his/her assistance.

SEATING

- Assist the elderly and baby first.
- Assist the lady guests by pulling out their chair. When they are seated, assist them by moving the chair into position.
- The lady should move nearer to the table herself, while allowing the host to assist her.

CHILDREN

- Children need to enjoy eating at a restaurant as the adults do. Children should always behave well and consider other guests.
- Children should not be allowed to run around in the restaurant, they must be taught to be seated for the duration of the meal. It could be dangerous if a child bumps into a waiter carrying hot food, beverages or glasses that might fall and break.
- Draw the attention of the waiter if you need a baby chair.
- Parents must order for the children. Children may only place their order with the permission of the person who is responsible for the bill.
- When the children are hungry, order their food first. Order something that will not take long to prepare.

BEVERAGES

- In most cases the wine steward will take the order for all the drinks. Make sure whether it must be paid for when the order is served or if it will be included in the bill for the meal.
- Beer is never a good choice to order before and during a meal, as it is very filling. If you have to wait for your table and you order something from the bar, you are allowed to take the glass to the table. Sometimes the waiter will assist you. A good choice is to order a dry or medium cream sherry before the meal.
- The host may order the wine, or ask the guests their preference. The wine steward will bring the bottle to the table for the host to make sure it is the wine he had ordered. The guests can also test the temperature of the wine, or smell the cork of the red wine bottle. The wine steward will pour a little into the glass of the host. He will taste the wine and signal to the waiter that he is satisfied. The waiter will pour wine for the rest of the guests and place the wine on ice.

GIVING THE ORDER TO THE WAITER

Study the menu and make your choice. Do not make the order complicated, order from the menu. Do not demand food that is not on the menu, e.g. do not order grilled steak from an exclusively seafood restaurant.

THE INVITED GUEST

When you are invited to a lunch or a dinner party at someone's house, basic etiquette still applies, but there are other etiquette rules to consider.

Always reply to an invitation as soon as possible. Make sure you are informed about the following:

DATE AND TIME

It is unacceptable to arrive too early, it could be an embarrassment to the hostess, as she might not be ready or prepared to accommodate the guests while still attending to last minute tasks. Never arrive late. To arrive too late, shows disrespect to the host as well as the rest of the guests. The hostess may excuse these bad manners but will think twice before you are invited again.

If you are invited, the invitation should stipulate if children are included. Never ask a hostess if you could bring friends along. This could be embarrassing to the hostess to have to say no and you might inconvenience her by having to cater for more people than she planned for. In some cases she might only have space for eight at her table and therefore prepared for eight settings. If you bring an uninvited friend, she has to make special arrangements.

DRESS CODE, FORMAL OR INFORMAL

If it is expected of you to dress formally, you will embarrass the hostess and yourself if you are not dressed accordingly.

GIFTS TO THE HOST OR HOSTESS

At an informal occasion it is allowed to enquire if there is something they wish you to contribute. If the answer is no, you may bring wine or flowers if you are familiar with their taste. It is not acceptable at a formal dinner to bring wine or flowers or any gift. It is a better choice to send a thank-you note with flowers or a well-chosen gift, not more than two days after the event to the hostess. If the hostess receives flowers, she has to put it in a vase immediately or give it to someone else to attend to, while she might have to attend to other guests as well. If you are the hostess, accept the gift with gratitude, but never put the flowers aside unattended.

When wine is given to the host or hostess, it is a gift and not to be served at the meal. Chocolates received as a gift, should not be shared with the guests but put away. The hostess should never neglect to thank the guest.

ARRIVAL

When the hostess invites you in, you should enter and wait upon the hostess to show you where to sit. You never invite yourself in and sit down where you want to or walk around in the house of the hostess.

WHEN TO START EATING

Always keep an eye on the host/hostess and follow what she/he is doing. If she places the serviette on her lap, you should follow and do the same. Never forget or ignore the serviette when it is set on the table. You have to put it on your lap and not only make use of it when you need it.

If the host/ess indicates that grace will be said, the needed respect should be shown. Start to eat after the host/ess has started eating. It is good to see that all the guests have been served before you start eating. Maintain a pace of eating to finish together with the rest of the guests.

COMMENTS ON FOOD

You should never express your likes or dislikes of food at table; it might just be what is prepared for you. Try not to refuse any food given by the hostess unless it is in direct conflict with your religion or if you are allergic to such food. If you dislike the food, eat a small portion, but try not to show your dislike. A compliment to the chef is always appreciated.

HYGIENE AT TABLE

The following is not acceptable and falls in bad taste:

Never clean your teeth at the table, not with a toothpick, your fingernail or with the cutlery. Even if you try to shield you mouth with your hand, it is not acceptable. Take a toothpick, excuse yourself from the table and clean your teeth in private, if it is needed. To some people it has become customary to clean their teeth after dinner at the table for all guests to tolerate or ignore. If you have to sneeze or cough, turn your face away from the table and the guests. Never blow your nose at the table, excuse yourself and do it in private.

Do not scratch yourself, e.g. face, nose, ear, hair at table, or make noises not acceptable.

SERVIETTE

You should always place your serviette on your lap when a serviette is set at the table.

Dub your mouth clean when needed with the serviette. Do not use the serviette to clean your nose or wipe the sweat from your face. When you leave the table, do not forget the serviette on your lap and allow it to slip to the floor. Do not fold the serviette when you leave the table, place it unfolded on the left side of the cover. If the serviette is folded neatly, it might be taken that the serviette is clean and not used. The serviette is never placed on the chair. The serviette might have food stains on it, which might stain the chair or the clothes if the seat is stained. Never lick your fingers. Use the serviette or the finger bowl. If you have made a mess, or have spilt something, asks the waiter for assistance, do not use your serviette, unless it is an emergency.

PASSING ON ITEMS AT THE TABLE

First see if the other guests are served. If not, pass the item to the other guests and then serve yourself. Salt and pepper is always passed as a set and not salt or pepper only. Place the item you pass on the table to prevent accidents, unless the guest reaches out to you to receive the item and it is safe to hand it over. When you need something out of your reach, do not stretch to reach it, rather ask the other guests to pass it on to you.

POSTURE AT THE TABLE

Sit up straight, not on the edge of the chair. Move your chair in under the table, in order to support your back at the back of the chair.

Do not move in such a manner that your back faces towards some of the guests, more so when you have a conversation with someone next to you.

Keep your hands on your lap when you are not eating and never put your elbows on the table.

Do not use the cutlery or point out or explain something during a conversation. Do not play or tap on the table with the cutlery.

HANDBAG AND CELLPHONE

Handbag hooks are convenient to hang your handbag onto the table. This is not always possible. You may place your bag next to you on the chair or hang it over the arm of the chair if possible. The last choice is to place your handbag on the floor, but never on the table.

The cellphone is to be switched off during meals and left in your bag or pocket. Only in exceptional cases and cases of emergency are you allowed placing the cell phone on the table and answering it during mealtime. To talk on the telephone while all the other guests are waiting to start eating, is showing disrespect to the rest of the guests.

EATING BREAD AT THE TABLE

Never make a sandwich at table. When e.g. bread is served with minced meat and eggs do not load the egg and minced meat onto the slice of bread and place another slice on top. Bread should be broken into bite sizes with your hands and eaten with the hand. To place bite size pieces of bread on the plate and eat it with the rest of the food, is allowed. One piece at a time is put on the plate and not the whole slice which is broken into pieces.

SECOND HELPINGS

At a formal dinner with more than one course, never ask for a second helping. This can only be done when your host/ess asks you if you would like a second helping.

Rather dish up smaller portions at a buffet and go for second helpings. If there is loads of food, it does not mean you have to overload your plate. It is only good manners to finish everything on your plate, unless you are satisfied before you have finished. It is not acceptable to dish up, eat half of the food and go for a second or third helping. Arrange the servings next to each other, not on top of one another. The only exception is when you pour gravy over your food. Accompaniments such as mustard, horseradish sauce, mint sauce e.g. is dished up next to the food you intend to eat with it.

Keep your eyes on the rest of the guests, so that you do not eat too slow or too fast. See that you finish with the rest of the group. If the waiter asks for your plate, indicate you are still busy eating, by placing your knife and fork horizontally on your plate.

CROCKERY AND CUTLERY

Never inspect cutlery or crockery or turn it to check the quality mark, or wipe it when it is stained. If it is not clean, ask the waiter, without making a fuss, to replace it.

Rest your hands on your lap when you are not eating. When the cover is not correctly set or not within your taste, do not change or correct it. If you are left handed, pick up the cutlery and change it to the other hand when your start eating. Do not lift a large piece of food from your plate with a fork and eat it bite by bite from the fork. Load your fork with a bite size of food.

Scoop sufficient food on your spoon so that you can finish it off with one bite; do not lick off the food bit by bit from the spoon.

Never lick your glass, cup, spoon, or fork or put the knife into your mouth.

USING A STRAW

At an informal occasion and at restaurants a straw is sometimes used, e.g. when drinking a milkshake. The straw should be removed from the glass when it is not used and the person is drinking from the glass.

Prevent making a noise with the straw by sucking when the glass is almost empty.

DRINKING FROM A BOTTLE

At a restaurant the drink should be poured into a glass. For informal occasions and outdoor entertainment, drinking from the bottle is allowed.

Do not use your personal cutlery for dishing up.

SERVING YOURSELF

Check the other guests and the amount of food served. E.g. if there are only six potatoes and six guests, you should not take two potatoes.

Place each portion next to the other portion and do not heap one portion on top of another portion. Only gravy, sauces and garnish are placed on top of food.

When other guests do not apply good table manners or the necessary etiquette, ignore it and pretend that you did not notice. Never try to correct a guest at a dinner table; you only correct your own children.

TAKING FOOD HOME

You do not help yourself with left overs and take it home when you did not pay for the food. If your hostess dishes up left overs for you to take it home, accept it gracefully and thank her, do not forget to take it home.

It is never permitted to take food home from a buffet table, not even your leftover food. When you brought food from home as your contribution to the meal, empty your container to take the container home but do not take the leftover food or you can collect your container later. It is a good gesture to present the container/dish as a gift.

CONVERSATION AT THE TABLE

At formal dinners, you only make conversation with the persons sitting next to you or opposite you if the table is not very wide.

At informal dinners conversation can take place with any of the guests. Never take over the conversation, give all guests an opportunity to participate. Determine what your guests interests are. Never become technical about topics of which your guests know nothing. Do not discuss other people or become personal. Ignore any topic that could make the other guests feel uncomfortable. Avoid conflict in all circumstances. Avoid talking about yourself or your personal money matters, how rich you are or were or will become. Avoid subjective matters and stay objective in any discussion.

SMOKING

Smoking is not allowed at the table. Guests have to excuse themselves from the table to smoke. Even if you could ask for permission from the host to smoke at the table, it is not done. The host and the rest of the guests will never refuse and will say nothing, but they have to tolerate and put up with the smoker at the table.

AFTER THE MEAL

Do not start scratching the leftover food from your plate and from the plates of the guests. Do not collect the other guest's plates and pile it up. Do not push your empty plate away from you when you have finished. Allow the host/ess to guide you as to what they expect from you. Do not ask to help. If she would give you a hint, you may ask to assist. Allow the waiter to remove the used plates and utensils.

Ladies may excuse themselves from the table to touch up their lipstick after the meal; it is not done at the table.

THE CORRECT METHOD OF HANDLING CUTLERY

AMERICAN STYLE

Food is cut into smaller portions with the knife and fork. The knife is placed at the top of the plate, cut side facing towards the inside of the plate. The fork is transferred to the right hand.

Hold the fork in the middle of the handle and not at the end. The tines should face upwards while eating.

CONTINENTAL STYLE

Knife and fork

When you eat with a knife and fork, the twines are always facing downwards and the food is scooped with the knife on the backside (round side) of the fork Do not hold the knife and fork in your fist or as if you are holding a pencil.

If you are right handed, scoop food onto the fork, knife in the right hand and fork in the left hand, when you are right handed.

Although food should be dished up with portions neatly placed next to another on the plate, foods may be mixed while scooping on the fork. Menus are set for different foods to complement each other and should be eaten together.

When dessert is eaten with a spoon and fork, the fork is used to guide the food onto the spoon or to secure the food while cutting a smaller portion with the spoon. The fork is used to clear the spoon underneath by holding the fork with the twines downwards and scraping from the front to the back of the spoon.

Basic Western Table Etiquette And Waiter Service

The position of your cutlery while you are still eating

The position of your cutlery when you have finished eating

C. THE BUSINESS LUNCH
EATING AT THE WORKPLACE

When you first start at a new place of employment, you have to observe the business policy pertaining eating at the workplace.

The rest of the employees will quickly guide you and tell you what is permitted and what not.

Do not eat during working hours. Do not keep food or morsels of food in your drawers or lying around on your desk. It is in bad taste to chew chewing gum while working and communicating with co-workers. Use your teatime and lunchtime for eating. If you are very busy, even so, take of a few minutes to eat and come back to your work. It would be an embarrassment for your superior to address you if your mouth is full of food or your hands are occupied holding the food or snack you intend to eat. You are stealing time from your employer when you eat outside of lunch hours and to wash your hands after eating. It might seem innocent, but when thinking of the implication thereof, it is altogether a no go during working hours to eat or snack.

ORGANIZE THE BUSINESS LUNCH

You have to determine the purpose of the business meal.

A business meal may be arranged to discuss a contract, a business deal or for the employer to evaluate his/her prospective employee.

According to the purpose of the meal, an "agenda" needs to be compiled, to be discussed at the meal.

Inform the person or persons concerned what is expected of them. This would include the date, time, venue, dress code and also important the guests invited.

Date

Make sure to invite the persons concerned well in advance so they can be well prepared.

Time

The time will determine whether it would be a lunch or dinner. There should be enough time to enjoy the meal at leisure as well as discuss the matters concerned.

Venue

When you invite the guest, make sure of the following:

Kind of restaurant

If you know your client or guest does not eat fish, do not book at the Ocean Basket that only serves fish.

The environment and atmosphere of the restaurant is as important. There should be enough privacy to be able to talk without the next table overhearing your conversation. Tables should not be too close together. The table you choose should not be near the entrance or restrooms or kitchen door where there is more movement than in other areas in the restaurant. A busy restaurant that caters for children and children's parties would hardly be appropriate for a business lunch. A restaurant with a loud band would also not be beneficial to promote communication. The table you choose should be large enough if at any stage you have to take out a computer or notes to explain something to your guest.

Regarding dress code, give guidelines as to what you would expect your guest to wear as some restaurant's dress code requires their guests to wear a jacket.

Guests

Your guest should be aware that it is a business lunch and not a family lunch. He or she will not be expected to bring along his/her spouse or children or extra guests.

Make the necessary arrangement beforehand with the restaurant

Inform the Maitre'd beforehand that you will take care Of the bill. Explain the purpose of the meal and ask for a table in an appropriate area of the restaurant. Arrange that the waiter should take your order and be around if needed, but not interrupt unnecessarily.

Be at the venue on time to greet your guest.

WHEN YOU ARE INVITED TO A BUSINESS LUNCH

You always have to adhere to the basic etiquette rules.

It could be a meeting for an important business transaction, be aware, your behaviour could just determine the outcome.

Any employer knows that an employee can make or break a business. Careful evaluation is needed when choosing an employee. It could happen that the final decision will be taken after a lunch or dinner.

EVALUATION AT THE BUSINESS LUNCH

Some of the following characteristics may surface and will be identified by an observant employer. The situation and circumstances at the meal might not reveal all the characteristics listed, but some might be obvious.

PUNCTUALITY

If you are late for the meal, it could be a sign that you are not organized.

It might indicate that you cannot plan and will not be fit for a position where you have to set an example or be responsible for any planning and decision making. It could also indicate that you do not show respect for other people's time. The employer cannot allocate important tasks to you where punctuality is important.

Just to phone and say you will be late is not at all acceptable.

Excuses such as that the traffic was hectic or any other excuses might indicate that you do not have the ability to make provision for possible unforeseen circumstances or to plan ahead.

BACKGROUND

Your background will show in the way you apply good manners or not. With good manners, you might be a good candidate in a management position or where you have to interact with clients.

HONESTY AND TRUSTWORTHINESS

Unfortunately honesty and trustworthiness sometimes only shows in the long run. Most important indicators at dinner could be any or more of the following situations: When condiments or after dinner mints are offered and you use more and in abundance than what are needed. It will be noticed when you slip toothpicks, sachets of sugar or other items into your bag or pocket. This is a sure sign that you will abuse and take advantage of office equipment e.g. use the computer at work for private use or take some stationary home. You will use your cell phone during working hours for private calls or take a few minutes longer for tea or lunch breaks. Using working time for your private affairs is a sure way of stealing. No employer wants to play policeman to his employees.

INTEGRITY

Integrity could surface in many areas during a meal. It could be revealed in your conversation with the employer and other guests. It will be a red flag if you criticize your previous employer or discuss private matters about your previous employer. You are not supposed to bring up money matters at the lunch. When you insinuate you have been underpaid, the employer might expect that you would soon start to complain about your salary. You would not be a good choice as the rest of the staff would soon be influenced by you.

There is a saying that money surfaces a person's character. Do not take it for granted that your employer, "because he can afford" it that he must pay for your meal. Ask if you could contribute or if it is declined, if you could pay the tip for the waiter who was so friendly or supportive. This will indicate you are not selfish, you do not take everything for granted, and that you are appreciative. A person who expects someone else to pay for his meal would not be a trustworthy person to employ. This person would always seek where he or she could benefit from the "company" which is so rich and he will soon feel underpaid or not valued in the long run.

If the salt and pepper canister is taken and dredged onto the food before tasting it, it could be seen as a sign of being impulsive.

COMMUNICATION SKILLS

It will be observed how well you listen and how well you react on questions asked. Signs at the table could be when this person takes over the conversation. This person will not be successful where orders need to be taken. When this person does not take note of all the other guests at the table and only wants to capture all the attention of the employer, it could be that he might seek favoritism. The following gestures would indicate poor communication skills: When this person is spoken to, and he does not show real interest, he does not make eye contact; his body language is not in line with his listening skills. E.g. when someone enters the restaurant, he looks away while in conversation to see who is entering, or he looks at his watch, or his eyes follow the waiter while being spoken to. When he sits with his arms folded, it also shows poor interest. You should sit up straight with your back against the back of the chair and your hands should be relaxed in your lap. When good communication skills are lacking this person will not be a good choice to give or receive orders. When the guest takes over the conversation it could be that this person will not easily submit in the work environment. It will be noticed if you as the guest is a good listener and evaluates situations and considers other people's inputs.

For a business lunch the dress code speaks for itself. See that you are dressed formally.

Don't start with business talk after the meals are served. The subordinate in the meeting should give the superior the opportunity to start business talk.

LEADERSHIP

For a leadership position, this person should have good communication skills.

This person must treat every person with respect. Leadership qualities will show in the way you treat the waiter. This person would immediately know what dish to order. He will be cautious not to order a dish which is difficult or messy to eat, such as spaghetti or unshelled prawns.

A person with good leadership skills will take the lead in caring when he sees an elderly person who needs assistance.

TEAMWORK

When you take over the conversation or interrupt the other guests and advise them what to order you will not be a good choice where teamwork is essential.

COMPATABILIY

Be careful not to draw the attention on yourself when any subject comes up. Although you might have more experience or knowledge in a certain field, never take over the conversation.

You should mind your language. Do not make use of "slang" or bad language in general. You will not be a good choice to work with clients

Compatibility might show when the guest orders something that is not on the menu. Will the guest get upset and insist or put the waiter at ease and immediately make another choice. The guest should not give orders to the waiter apart outside the waiter's job description or behave badly by being rude or bossy to the waiters. To give orders to the waiter would be the task of the person who pays the bill, unless this person invites you to order. The way you interact with the waiter will also show how well or not, you are in control or treat difficult situations. This could also be an indication of how you would treat your co-workers.

ATTITUDE

A positive attitude is an asset to any employer.

It will be noticed if the guest treats the waiter with impatience. A bad attitude will also show when the guest is friendly with the host, and unfriendly with the other guests.

Sit up straight with your back against the back of the chair and not on the tip of your chair, or slouch in the chair. This definitely is a sign of laziness, disrespect or arrogance. Do not fold your arms when you are not eating, but keep them relaxed on your lap. Folded arms may indicate that you are not really interested in what is going on at the table.

DEDICATION

When the guest takes the salt, sprinkles his food without tasting it first, could be seen as impulsiveness.

RESPONSIBILITY

At a business meal, you must be disciplined and switch off your cell phone. When the cellphone rings and you excuse yourself every time, it is a sign of poor discipline.

The prospective employee will give the employer a good idea of how controlled he is when it comes to the use of alcohol. At a business lunch it is best not to order any alcoholic beverages. Should he ignore the law and drink too much, when he knows he still has to drive home, or return to the office, it could be a sign that he would not mind not to observe the company policy as well.

CONFLICT SOLVING

This characteristic could only be detected when a conflict situation occurs at the table. What method did you apply to solve a conflict situation?

When the music is too loud or the table where you sit is very noisy, how would you address the situation and that could determine what a good problem solver you are. The best way to solve such a problem would be to excuse yourself and ask the waiter to ask the superior to turn the music down or move the party to another table. It would not be your place to ask the waiter to turn the music down in front of the all other guests. It would not be good if you sit and complain about the noisiness and criticize the management of the restaurant.

SELFISHNESS

When the guest starts to eat immediately after his food is served, without waiting for the other guests to be served, it is a sign of selfishness. The guest must keep an eye on the rest of the guests and notice if they need something e.g. passing the salt, or condiments.

While enjoying the lunch, be alert and observant of the needs of the other guests. This will show that you care for other people and they are important to you, because you value them and take care of their needs.

Consider the needs of others around you especially with items within your reach.

BEING AN ASSET AS AN EMPLOYEE

When the guest smokes after each course, which is of course not acceptable, the employer will quickly determine how many hours he has to pay this employee for all his smoke breaks.

The guest should not give orders to the waiter outside of the waiter's job description or behave badly by being rude or bossy to the waiters. To give orders to the waiter would be the task of the person who pays the bill, unless this person invites you to order. The way you interact with the waiter will also show how well or not, you are in control of treating difficult situations. This could also be an indication how you would treat your co-workers. A troublemaker would not be an asset in the workplace because time is wasted by having to sort out problems with staff members.

BIBLIOGRAPHY

1. CM Nel, JS Heyns, RC Bouer, HOME ECONOMICS IN ACTION ST 6, 7, 8. JUTA Publishers Cape Town SA 1986
2. E Nawrotski, RC Bouer, HOME ECONOMICS IN ACTION ST 9, 10. JUTA Publishers Cape Town SA 1988
3. Charlotte Ford, BOOK OF MODERN MANNERS, Fireside Publishers 1982
4. Amy van der Bilt, COMPLETE BOOK OF ETIQUETTE, Doubleday Publishers 1995

THE AUTHOR

Rachel (Ralie) Bouer, (Spray) was a lecturer and Head of the Home Economics Department at a Teacher's Training College in Pretoria. She was co-author of 5 Home Economics textbooks, Grade 8 to 12. She was an external examiner for Home Economics teachers for Education and Training in all the provinces. She served on the Home Economics study group and study committees. She also served as judge for the "VLU". (Cooking and needlework). She has furthered her studies in business and exports. Presently she is running her own company Cum Laude and lecturing Bible Colleges.

Dr R C Bouer

MAIL THIS APPLICATION FORM WITH YOUR ANSWERING SHEET TO THE ADDRESSS BELOW

TO: **WAITER AND ETIQUETTE COURSE**
THE EXAMINER
P.O.BOX 3714
BRITS NORTH WEST S.A. 0250

TEL NO: 012 2500085. e-mail-your application and answer sheet to : rcbouer@live.co.za. Postage for the certificate will be required.

YOUR STUDENT NUMBER:

ONLY AN ORIGINAL COPY FROM THE BOOK WITH THE CANDIDATE'S NUMBER QUALIFIES. Candidates must be older than 16 years.

You will receive your results as well as a Certificate of completion of the basic waiter course, within 21 working days after evaluation.

COURSE: ETIQUETTE & WAITER REGISTRATION & APPLICATION:

NAME:..
I.D. No: ....
Address: ....
....
Highest Qualification:...
Tel No:..

ANSWER SHEET:
NAME: _____
MAXIMUM MARKS 100
TOTAL MARKS: _____

Answer the question by crossing the corresponding symbol to your answer e.g. a b c d e f (1), or where more marks are indicated, more crossings e.g. a b c d e f (4)

1.	A	B	C	D	(1)
2.	A	B	C	D	(1)
3.	A	B	C	D	(1)
4.	A	B	C	D	(1)
5.	A	B	C	D	(1)
6.	A	B	C	D	(1)
7.	A	B	C	D	(1)
8.	A	B	C	D	(1)
9	A	B	C	D	(1)
10.	A	B	C	D	(1)
11.	A	B	C	D	(1)
12.	A	B	C	D	(1)
13.	A	B	C	D	(1)

14.	A	B	C	D	(1)
15.	A	B	C	D	(1)
16	A E	B F	C	D	(3)
17.	A E	B F	C	D	(3)

18	18.1	A	B	C	D	E	(1)
	18.2	A	B	C	D	E	(1)
	18.3	A	B	C	D	E	(1)
	18.4	A	B	C	D	E	(1)
	18.5	A	B	C	D	E	(1)
19.		A	B	C	D		(1)
20	20.1	A	B	C	D	E	(1)
	20.2	A	B	C	D	E	(1)
	20.3	A	B	C	D	E	(1)
	20.4	A	B	C	D	E	(1)
	20.5	A	B	C	D	E	(1)
21.		A	B	C	D		(1)
22.		A	B	C	D		(1)
23		A	B	C	D		(1)
24		A	B	C	D		(1)
25		A F	B G	C H	D I	E J	(5)
26		A	B	C	D		(1)

27		A	B	C	D		(1)
28		A	B	C	D		(1)
29		A	B	C	D		(1)
30		A	B	C	D		(1)
31		A	B	C	D		(1)
32		A	B	C	D		(1)
33		A	B	C	D		(1)
34		A	B	C	D		(1)
35		A	B	C	D		(1)
36		A	B	C	D		(1)
37		A	B	C	D		(1)

Answer your 4 long questions on separate sheets of paper. It might be typed or in your own handwriting.

REQUIREMENTS FOR QUALIFICATION:

TOTAL MARKS 100 (MINIMUM TO BE OBTAINED 70)

ANSWER THE FOLLOWING QUESTIONS BY CROSSING A, B OR C IN YOUR ANSWERING SHEET

1. **Incorrect clothing for the waiter could:**
   a) Be loose fitting
   b) Be out of fashion
   c) Dip into the food
   d) Draw the attention of customers

2. **Too much jewelry and bracelets are not allowed as it:**
   a) Draw too much attention
   b) Is too noisy
   c) Is too shiny
   d) Is too smart

3. **You are not allowed to serve guests when you:**
   a) Are tired
   b) Are unhappy
   c) Have a headache
   d) Have flu

4. **The waiter should wash his hands after he has:**
   a) Handled money
   b) Passed cutlery to a client
   c) Served alcoholic drinks
   d) Passed crockery to a client

5. **When serving beverages the waiter should stand on the:**

a) Left side of the guest, serving with the right hand
b) Right side of the guest, serving with the right hand
c) Left side of the guest, serving with the left hand
d) Right side of the guest, serving with the left hand

6. **The term "protocol" is used to describe good manners at:**
   a) Banquets
   b) Business meals
   c) State dinners
   d) Travelling

7. **At this kind of meal you may not ask for a second helping:**
   a) American style
   b) Banquet
   c) Buffet
   d) Russian

8. **At this kind of serving you dish up food for yourself and sit at a set table and eat**
   a) American style
   b) Buffet
   c) French
   d) Russian

9. **At this method of entertaining guests are standing and the party usually lasts not longer than two hours:**
   a) American
   b) Buffet
   c) Cocktail
   d) English service

10. **At this method of entertaining you should never eat with your hands:**
    - a) Banquette
    - b.) Buffet
    - c.) Cocktail
    - d.) Cheese & Wine

11. **At this method of serving the Chef de rang prepares the food at the table in front of the guest:**
    - a.) American
    - b.) Banquette
    - c.) Cocktail
    - d) French

12. **At this method of serving food is eaten with small forks, on toothpicks or by hand:**
    - a) American
    - b.) Banquette
    - c.) Cocktail
    - d) French

13. **The main reason why waiter should know the kind of ingredients used in a dish to inform his guests:**
    - a) Allergy of guest
    - b.) Color of the ingredient
    - c.) Interesting
    - d) Price of the food

14. **When an "a la Carte menu" is used;**
    - a) All foods listed are served at one price
    - b.) Guests pay separately for each listed dish

15. **A slow method of cooking:**
    - a) Baking
    - b.) Frying
    - c.) Steaming
    - Stewing

16. Cooking methods where oil is used:
a) Deep frying
b) Sauté
c) Steaming
d) Stew
e) Broiling
f) Braising

17. Dry methods of cooking:
a) Baking
b) Roasting
c) Broiling
d) Stewing
e) Steaming
f) Simmering

18. Match the food with its accompaniment
Example: 18.6-g

18.1 Apple Sauce   a) Pork
18.2 Mint Sauce   b) Roasted Beef
18.3 Sour cream   c) Mutton
18.4 Tartar Sauce   d) Baked potatoes
18.5 Yorkshire Pudding   e) Fish

19. A serviette is used to
a) Wipe your mouth
b) Dub your mouth
c) Wipe off sweat
d) Clean your fork & knife

20. Match the utensil used for each dish
20.1 Blunt knife   a) Eat bacon & eggs
20.2 Butter knife   b) Scoop butter into your side plate

20.3 Dessert knife   c) Spread butter and jam on your toast
20.4 Serrated knife   d) Eat fish
20.5 Table knife   e) Eat Steaks

21. When you use this spoon you sip from the side of the spoon
 a) Dessert-spoon
 b) Soup-spoon
 c) Table-spoon
 d) Tea-spoon

22. The bottle with this beverage must be placed in the ice bucket when opened:
 a) Brandy
 b) Red wine
 c) White wine
 d) Whisky

23. White wine glasses should be filled:

 a) 1/3
 b) 2/3
 c) ½
 d) Filled to the brim

24. Red wine glasses should be filled
 a) 1/3
 b) 2/3
 c) ½
 d) Full

25. The purpose of a doily under the tea cup is to
 a) Absorb excess moisture
 b) Be smart
 c) Dampen noise
 d) Match the color scheme

Basic Western Table Etiquette And Waiter Service

26. **List 5 important items you could expect to be on a side stander:**
    - a) Biscuits
    - b) Cheese
    - c) Extra napkins
    - d) Glasses
    - e) Knife & fork
    - f) Mustard
    - g) Order pads
    - h) Sugar
    - i) Table cloths
    - j) Used utensils

27. **These persons' function is to remove used utensils**
    - a) Busboy
    - b) Chef
    - c) Chef de rang
    - d) Commis de rang

28. **When presenting the menu the waiter should stand at:**
    - a) Behind the guest
    - b) In front of the guest
    - c) The left side of the guest
    - d) The right side of the guest

29. **Used utensils are removed from this side of the guest:**
    - a) Front
    - b) Left

c) Right

30. Beverages are served from this side of the guest:
a) Front
b) Left
c) Right

31. When removing the used utensils:
a) Ask guests to pass it on
b) Remove as many plates you possibly can at a time
c) Remove only two or maximum 3 plates at a time
d) Scrap the plates clean at the table

32. When you serve guests with children:
a) Do not serve them full glasses and piping hot beverages
b) Ignore the children
d) Take the children away and take care of them when they become difficult
c) Take an order from the children

33. A drink usually served with fish:
a) Beer
b) Port
c) Red wine
d) White wine

34. A drink usually served with venison
  a) Brandy
  b) Cocktail
  c) Red wine
  d) White wine

35. A drink usually served after the meal:
  a) Beer
  b) Port
  c) Red wine
  d) Sherry

36. A drink usually served before the meal:
  a) Beer
  b) Port
  c) Red wine
  d) Sherry

37. At large restaurants this person meets the guests at the entrance sand show them their table:

  a) Commis de rang
  b) Busboy
  c) Waiter
  d) Maitre'd

38. You can identify the fish knife, as it is:
  a) Blunt
  b) Larger than the dessert knife
  c) Serrated edge
  d) Very sharp

39. How would you identify the soup spoon:
  a) Long handle
  b) Round wand wide scoop
  c) Serrated on the point of the spoon
  d) Smaller than the desert-spoon

Evaluation Notes:

Write notes on issues you are not sure of, pertaining etiquette:

a) In general 5   b) Table etiquette   10

Write notes on issues most irritating during   5
restaurant service

Write etiquette notes on your own culture at   10
mealtime.

Write a complete job description for a waiter.   25

Total   **100**

Index

A

AMERICAN SERVICE 42
ANSWERING THE TELEPHONE 17

B

BANQUET SERVICE 35
BASIC RESPONSIBILITIES (JOB DESCRIPTION) 14
BEHAVIOUR OF A WAITER 6
BUFFET/(SMORGASBORD) 37

C

COCKTAIL PARTIES AND CHEESE AND WINE PARTIES 43
COMMUNICATION SKILLS 9
COOKING METHODS 48

D

DIFFERENT KINDS OF (SERVING) ENTERTAINMENT 35

E

EATING AT THE WORKPLACE 90
EVALUATION AT THE BUSINESS LUNCH 93

F

FAMILY STYLE SERVING 36
FRENCH STYLE SERVICE 39

I

IMPORTANT INFORMATION FOR THE WAITER 46

M

MEETING GUESTS AT THE ENTRANCE OF THE RESTAURANT 18

N

NON-DISCRIMINATION 10

O

ORGANIZE THE BUSINESS LUNCH 91

P

PREPARATION BEFORE OPENING 14

R

RUSSIAN SERVICE 40

S

SAFETY AND SECURITY 12
SERVING TEA 44
SERVING THE GUESTS 20
SETTING THE TABLE 52
SPECIAL ATTENTION 32
SPREADING OF DISEASE 11

T

TABLE ETIQUETTE FOR EVERYONE 75
TEAMWORK 6
THE BUSINESS LUNCH 90
THE HISTORY OF ETIQUETTE 1
THE INVITED GUEST 78
THE MENU 47
THE RESTAURANT GUEST 75
THE WAITER 2
TRUST AND HONESTY 10

www.ingramcontent.com/pod-product-compliance
Lightning Source LLC
Chambersburg PA
CBHW021544200526
45163CB00015B/1229